Protecting Young Children from Sexual Abuse

Protecting Young Children from Sexual Abuse

Does Preschool Training Work?

Neil Gilbert
Jill Duerr Berrick
Nicole Le Prohn
Nina Nyman
Family Welfare Research Group,
University of California at Berkeley

Lexington Books
D.C. Heath and Company/Lexington, Massachusetts/Toronto

Library of Congress Cataloging-in-Publication Data

Protecting young children from sexual abuse : does preschool training work? /
Neil Gilbert . . . [et al.].
    p.   cm.
    Includes bibliographies.
    ISBN 0-669-20103-0 (alk. paper)
    1. Child molesting—Prevention—Study and teaching (Preschool)—California.
I. Gilbert, Neil, 1940–
HQ72.U53P79   1989   362.7'1—dc19

Published simultaneously in Canada
Printed in the United States of America
International Standard Book Number: 0-669-20103-0
Library of Congress Catalog Card Number: 88-30302

The paper used in this publication meets the minimum requirements of American National
Standard for Information Sciences—Permanence of Paper for Printed Library Materials,
ANSI Z39.48-1984. ∞™

89 90 91 92 8 7 6 5 4 3 2 1

Contents

Figures

Tables

Acknowledgments

This book is based on a study conducted by the Family Welfare Research Group of the School of Social Welfare, University of California at Berkeley, under a grant from the National Center on Child Abuse and Neglect, Department of Health and Human Services. During the course of the study our work benefited from the generous assistance of numerous colleagues and organizations, to whom we would like to extend our warmest appreciation. Deborah Daro played an important role in the planning, design, and initial stages of research implementation. Linda Reese, Beth Hardesty Fife, Dave Foster, and Bob Green at the Office of Child Abuse Prevention, California State Department of Social Services, offered continuous encouragement and the kind of bureaucratic support that made it possible for us to launch a statewide project. At various stages of our project we were challenged and aided by the thoughtful criticism and helpful advice of Jon Conte, James Garbarino, Frances Stott, Sally Cooper Woods, Jane Hunt and her staff at the University of California at Berkeley Child Study Center, members of the Langley Porter Institute, and Meryl Glass and her staff at the Child Care Study Center of the University of California, San Francisco. Finally, this study could not have been completed without the cooperation of a highly dedicated group of child abuse prevention service providers, among whom we owe a special thanks to Kate Kain, Brenda Blasingame, Pnina Tobin, Sue Levinson Farley, Sherri Patterson, Pat Osborne, Laura McMahon, Barrie Levy, Daryl Taylor, and JoAnne Rhudy. While the constructive criticism and good advice of all these colleagues helped to sharpen and improve our analysis of child abuse prevention efforts, we must, of course, accept the final responsibility for whatever deficiencies remain in this work.

Some of the findings from this study have been published in *The Public Interest* and the *International Journal of Child Abuse and Neglect*. We thank these journals for permission to incorporate portions of those articles in this book.

Some of the findings from this study have been published in Neil Gilbert, "Preventing Sexual Abuse," *The Public Interest* 93 (Fall 1988):3–15 and Jill Duerr Berrick, "Parental Involvement in Child Abuse Prevention Training: What Do They Learn?" *International Journal of Child Abuse and Neglect* 12, No. 4 (Fall 1988):543–553. Permission to reprint has been granted.

Introduction

C hild abuse is a grave problem, the exact depths of which are difficult to gauge. Between 1972 and 1984 the number of suspected child abuse cases reported to the authorities more than doubled from 610,000 to 1.5 million. These figures represent only part of the problem, since many if not most incidents of child abuse are never reported to public authorities. Not to exaggerate the case, however, interpretation of the official figures must be tempered in view of the increasing rate of unsubstantiated reports, which climbed from 35 percent in 1975 to 65 percent in 1984.[1] Unsubstantiated reports involve incidents in which guilt is not proven, a verdict falling rather short of not guilty. While the full measure of this problem is elusive, no matter how one reads the numbers, the more than one-half million substantiated cases in 1984 represent an immense scale of human suffering.

With the establishment of the National Center on Child Abuse and Neglect under the Child Abuse Prevention and Treatment Act of 1974, the federal government joined its resources to ongoing state and local efforts in the long-standing struggle against child abuse. Since the mid-1970s, there has been a proliferation of child abuse prevention initiatives throughout the country. Crisis hot lines, family counseling, perinatal and prenatal services, out-of-home placements, in-home supports, respite care, and education are among the varied activities typically funded for purposes of child abuse prevention. Many of these activities prevent abuse only in the sense of inhibiting its recurrence—that is, they are more ameliorative and curative than preventive as this term is commonly understood. Some of the activities, however, are devoted to prevention in its primary sense, a principal example of which are educational programs for children.

Over the past decade a virtual industry has sprung up around child abuse prevention courses. Books, curricula, videos, and an array of educational paraphernalia such as anatomically correct dolls, puppets, and posters have been produced for use in numerous programs supported by state and local governments across the nation. Leading the way, California has implemented the largest and most comprehensive child abuse prevention education program in the country. Under the Child Abuse Prevention Training Act of 1984 (CAPTA), the state provides about $11 million annually for "age-appropriate training in preschool, once during kindergarten, and at least three times during a child's school career in grades 1 through 12."[2] The training programs include parent and teacher workshops as well as classroom instruction for children.

While these programs are supposed to cover the full range of abusive and neglectful behavior, in practice they focus most on the prevention of sexual abuse. There are a number of reasons for this emphasis. From the early 1970s to the present reports of child sexual assault increased at an alarming rate. In California, for example, reports of sexual abuse climbed 490 percent between 1982 and 1986.[3] The growing public concern about this problem has been stirred by intense media coverage of several chilling cases of preschool children being sexually assaulted in day-care programs. Also, victims of child sexual assault often do not exhibit physical signs of maltreatment, making identification of these cases more problematic than those involving physical abuse and serious neglect.

In response to the growing public concern about sexual abuse of children, the CAPTA was passed by the California legislature with overwhelming support. This support expressed a serious wish to protect the young and vulnerable. Although at the time legislators were probably unclear about what should be conveyed in the classroom to help prevent sexual abuse, particularly in regard to preschool children, they were impelled to take some positive action. This book examines how that action came about and its consequences for preschool children.

In studying the California experience of child abuse prevention training at the preschool level, our analysis focuses on (1) the sociopolitical background of the CAPTA; (2) the curricula design and philosophy of seven prevention programs throughout the state; (3) the impact of these programs on children and parents; and (4) the curricula content in light of cognitive development and normative considerations. The final chapter explores the issues raised by this analysis and their implications for change. This investigation was undertaken in the hope that policymakers assessing the cost and social benefits of statewide child abuse prevention training at the preschool level and parents contemplating their children's participation in these programs will find the California experience instructive.

Notes

1. Douglas Besharov, "Unfounded Allegations—A New Child Abuse Problem," *Public Interest* (Spring 1986): 83, 18–33.

2. Chapter 12 of Welfare and Institutions Code, 18978.2(b), as amended by A.B.147.

3. Henry Miller, "The Social Ecology of Child Abuse" (Paper prepared for the Family Welfare Research Group, University of California, Berkeley. March, 1988).

1
California's Commitment to Prevention: From Idea to Statute

with *Allison Zippay*

T he Child Abuse Prevention Training Act (CAPTA), implemented in July 1985, appropriates $11 million annually for in-school primary prevention programs to children throughout the state of California. Under this act, children are offered prevention training five times in their school careers, from preschool through high school. Concurrent prevention workshops also are provided to the students' parents and teachers. As such, the bill stands as the most comprehensive piece of child abuse prevention legislation in the country. How and why did this landmark legislation develop? How was the program model chosen? What organizational efforts were required to effect its legislative passage? Why were California policymakers inclined to commit such a significant appropriation to in-school prevention programming?

The Evolution of a Prevention Bill

The CAPTA was drafted in the office of Assemblywoman Maxine Waters in the fall of 1983 and signed into law by Governor George Deukmejian one year later on September 29, 1984.[1] Introduced as Assembly Bill (AB) 2443, it was amended as AB 147 and implemented in July 1985. The bill's rapid progress from idea to statute met little public or legislative resistance on the way. Its movement was fueled by an advantageous combination of actors and circumstances, including the fact that it was an issue in the public and political spotlight, it had a strong legislative author, and it had committed, well-organized sponsors representing a broad-based, grass-roots child advocacy constituency.

The Issue: Spotlight on Child Abuse

In 1981 California revised its child abuse reporting laws, broadening both the class of persons mandated to report suspected cases of abuse and the requirements for those reports. Whereas mandated child abuse reporters previously had been limited mainly to physicians, they now included a broad array of professions ranging from therapists, teachers, and health professionals to commercial film developers. The language of the law was enlarged to require reports of reasonable suspicion as opposed to just known cases of abuse, and types of conduct considered abusive were expanded to include neglect, sexual assault, and willful cruelty, as well as nonaccidental physical injury.

Between 1980 and 1982 reports of child abuse in the state had climbed 22 percent from 97,000 to 120,000.[2] The increasing number of child abuse reports was amplified by extensive coverage by the media. Stories of child rape, molestation, disappearance, and kidnapping began receiving feature coverage both nationally and locally. In California such reporting turned into a blitz following a series of notorious kidnapping and abuse cases occurring from 1982 through 1984. These cases included the kidnapping of three-year-old Tara Burke from a shopping center in suburban Concord, the disappearance of eight-year-old Kevin Collins on his way home from school in San Francisco, and the exposure of the physical, sexual, and emotional abuse of dozens of preschoolers at the McMartin School in Manhattan Beach. Such coverage intensified public awareness and anxiety over the issue of child abuse. A collective nerve had been struck; all children were vulnerable whatever their age, class, race, or geographic locale. Parents, newspaper editors, and community leaders expressed concern that something more be done. Child advocates were pressing for front-end or prevention programs in addition to increased treatment and correctional services.

Representing these advocates, the California Consortium of Child Abuse Councils drafted a general child abuse prevention bill in 1981. Sponsored by Assemblyman Louis Papan, AB 1733 was signed into law in September 1982 with an annual appropriation of $10 million. The bill distributed funds on a per capita basis to counties, which in turn contracted with various local, community-based organizations to provide a variety of prevention efforts ranging from family counseling to special law enforcement services. With the wave of interest in child abuse yet to crest, AB 1733 established the amenability of politicians to child abuse prevention legislation. As abuse statistics and media attention continued to rise, so did legislative interest. In 1984 twenty-nine bills related to issues of child abuse were introduced to the legislature, one of which was the Maxine Waters Child Abuse Prevention and Training Act.

The Author: Assemblywoman Maxine Waters

Assemblywoman Maxine Waters has served in the California legislature since 1976. She represents south central Los Angeles, the Forty-Eighth Assembly District, covering Watts, Lynwood, and Southgate. A powerful and influential member of the assembly, she chairs the Democratic Caucus and serves on the Ways and Means, Judiciary, and Governmental Organization Committees.

Assemblywoman Waters has a history of supporting and sponsoring legislation affecting women, minorities, and youths. She is known as a tenacious and eloquent promoter of human rights.

Child abuse prevention was one of a number of issues Waters suggested to her legislative assistant, Stan DiOrio, in the summer of 1983 as potential material for an assembly bill. Waters traces her interest in child abuse prevention to the 1960s, when she was employed as a social worker in a Head Start program. Observing the complex developmental problems of abused children, she notes that she "came away with a heightened sense of the importance of a holistic social program approach to child welfare; one that included prevention as well as treatment."[3]

In 1983 the issue of child abuse prevention appeared politically ripe. Various legislators were working on bills addressing treatment issues; prevention was relativley untouched. Following Assemblywoman Waters's directions, DiOrio began to search the state for extant prevention models on which a bill could be based, as well as sponsors interested in taking on organizational and lobbying efforts. His inquiries led to a group of prevention practitioners whom he and Assemblywoman Waters found to have the requirements for a successful assembly bill campaign: a structured, easily replicable program model; experience with thirty prevention programs already operating in counties across California; vivid success stories; broad-based community support; and committed, articulate program organizers. The group was the Child Assault Prevention (CAP) Training Center of Northern California headed by Kate Kain and Rich Snowden.

*The Sponsors: The Child Assault
Prevention Training Center
of Northern California*

The CAP Training Center of Northern California was organized in the spring of 1981 by Kate Kain and Rich Snowden to train community volunteers in child abuse prevention methods. Both Kain and Snowden had previously worked in the area of rape crisis intervention and violence against women. Their project originated as an effort aimed at the prevention of child sexual assault. The program model used by the training center was initially developed and implemented in the mid-1970s by the Child Assault Prevention Project (CAPP) of Women Against Rape in Columbus, Ohio. The CAPP model uses skits and dialogue to teach children how to deal with potentially abusive situations. The approach is directed toward empowering children to recognize their basic right to be safe, strong, and free, instructing them in a variety of assertive, self-protective responses to abuse. The program also provides children with an opportunity to talk privately about the workshop material and disclose abuse. In addition, parent and teacher workshops on the CAPP methods are offered prior to child classroom presentations. With its structured curriculum, the CAPP model is relatively easy to demonstrate and replicate.

CAPP programs are usually coordinated through private, nonprofit community service organizations. Permission for in-school presentations is secured by the organization through local school administrators. The CAPP workshops are generally presented by volunteer community instruction teams.

Initially publicizing their model through the local network of rape crisis centers, the CAP Training Center of Northern California instructed its first group of community volunteers in the CAPP approach in the summer of 1981. Two years later, CAPP programs were being presented to children in thirty locales throughout California. The project's rapid spread was spurred by the strong organizing efforts of an enthusiastic and committed CAP Training Center staff and their swelling ranks of community instructors. As its use increased, the program quickly developed broad-based grass-roots support among parents, school personnel, and children's advocates.

In the fall of 1983, Stan DiOrio phoned Kate Kain to discuss the possibility of a child abuse prevention bill incorporating the CAPP model. The bill could potentially expand CAPP into a comprehensive, statewide system of prevention programs, as well as provide funding for what was then a meagerly financed, largely voluntary prevention network. It was agreed that the CAP Training Center would sign on as a sponsor of a child abuse prevention training bill.

Drafting the Bill

The initial draft of the CAPTA was pieced together by Stan DiOrio, Kate Kain, Rich Snowden, Linda Almdale (then president of the California Consortium of Child Abuse Councils), and Jane Callahan (legislative chair of the consortium). Both Almdale and Callahan had worked on AB 1733 and had agreed to lend their legislative expertise to AB 2443.

In its first round, the bill called for a state mandated prevention program to be administered in-school to all California children four times in their school careers—once each in preschool, elementary school, junior high school, and high school. The description of the mandated prevention program was based on the CAPP model. It was designed to include information and training concerning the right of every child to live free of abuse, the disclosing of incidents of abuse, the availability of support resources, child safety training and self-defense techniques, and private time for child counseling or reporting immediately following the workshop. The program was to be administered by the state Office of Child Abuse Prevention (OCAP), which would contract and fund the child abuse prevention programs. Workshops were to be culturally, linguistically, and geographically appropriate. To ensure adequate rural participation, counties were guaranteed a minimum $10,000 appropriation. The bill also prescribed the creation of two prevention training centers, one each in northern and southern California, which would provide information and other services to primary prevention programs. The legislation carried a price tag of $22 million annually.

The language of the bill was quite specific. Assemblywoman Waters had wanted legislation in which there was no ambiguity concerning what was to be funded. Everything was spelled out, from the prevention training curriculum to the requirements of training center applicants to the details of fiscal allocation. Specifics were negotiated among the bill's drafters, juggling political, practical, and philosophical considerations. The provision for training programs in preschool, elementary school, junior high school, and high school was based on the fact that abuse occurs at all ages and on the belief that assimilation of the material and disclosure of abuse was likely to increase with a repetition of instruction over the course of several years. The inclusion of preschool children in the program was based on statistics reflecting the vulnerability of very young children to abuse and a belief among prevention practitioners that preschool children were less likely to hold secrets and more likely to disclose abusive incidents. The programs were to be classroom based, where children could be reached most easily. A comprehensive statewide approach was proposed because of both the author's and the sponsor's belief in the efficacy of a blanket of prevention training made available to all children in the state.

Although workshops would be given to students' parents and teachers, the program was to be specifically child centered. As Assemblywoman Waters maintained, other bills or programs could address issues such as the training of parents at risk of abuse or the in-depth training of school personnel; AB 2443 was to be focused and directed toward the education of children. With draft in hand, the author and sponsors launched a campaign to organize community support and begin political lobbying around the bill.

Galvanizing Support

Community support was organized by the bill's sponsors, Kate Kain and Rich Snowden, joined by Gloviell Rowland from the Multicultural Coordination Council (MCC). MCC is a statewide network of groups and individuals who promote multicultural awareness in the design and implementation of social services for families and children, including child abuse prevention services. MCC was brought on as a second bill sponsor to represent the state's minority population and to secure support from child abuse prevention programs operating in southern California. Gloviell Rowland had been an assistant professor of psychology at Fuller Theological Seminary in Pasadena and was working on postdoctoral research at the University of California, Los Angeles (UCLA) in the area of child development and child abuse. Rowland also was a born-again Christian with a claim to a divine message to pursue work in the area of child abuse prevention. In the fall of 1983 she phoned Stan DiOrio to relay the specifics of her inspiration and became involved in the organizational work of AB 2443. The organization of community support for the bill was in the hands of two groups of prevention enthusiasts: Kain and Snowden, who were committed to the expansion of CAPP training programs, and Rowland, who was ardently pursuing a spiritual as well as a professional incentive in the area of child abuse prevention.

To organize their constituency, Kain and Snowden systematically mobilized participants in the thirty CAPP programs across the state. Each program director received a letter and phone call. The proposed bill was outlined, as were sample letters of endorsement for mailing to legislators. Local program organizers were asked to solicit and gather letters of support from parents, teachers, children, police officers, school administrators, and other community members familiar with the CAPP program. Program organizers also were asked to identify persons who would make impressive witnesses at committee hearings on the bill and to collect and write up success stories resulting from their program. In addition, it was suggested that word of the bill be spread through letters to local newspapers and dicussions at community meetings such as the Parent-Teacher Association (PTA) and church groups. A similar organizational effort was carried out by Rowland and the MCC in the southern part of the state. Persons working in the field of child abuse prevention were systematically notified of the bill and ways in which they could participate in the lobbying efforts. Letters and phone calls were directed to legislators, and word of the legislation spread to media and community members.

A basic tenet of community organization holds that community members will work for a cause in which they can identify a self-interest. AB 2443 was presented to local prevention program organizers as a mechanism through which their programs and personnel might secure significant, ongoing funding. The potential for increased revenues—in conjunction with a commitment to the importance of child abuse prevention programs—helped fuel local organizational efforts. Letters from parents, children, teachers, and community members in support of AB 2443 in general and the CAPP model in particular poured into legislative offices. Indeed, the staff personnel requested supporters to please signal their constituencies to slow their correspondence.

Political Strategy

While advocates set about organizing the grass roots, Stan DiOrio, with Callahan, Almdale, Kain, and Snowden, prepared a strategy to facilitate the bill's progress through the legislature. As previously noted, the CAPTA was one of twenty-nine bills related to issues of child abuse introduced to the legislature in 1984. The bills were collectively presented to the legislature as the 1984 Democratic Legislative Child Abuse Package. In 1983, Assemblyman Frank Vicencia, chair of the Assembly Select Committee on Child Abuse charged with developing a series of recommendations for reducing statewide incidence of abuse, had collected legislative proposals on the issue from Democratic senators and assemblypersons. The bills were an ad hoc batch, ranging from the expansion of categories of persons required to report child abuse (AB 2702) to the increase of marriage license fees to fund domestic violence centers (SB 1364). The package did not represent the result of a systematic assessment and evaluation of child abuse prevention and treatment problems and needs. Rather, it was a strategy employed to encourage the formulation of diverse legislative initiatives on the timely topic of child abuse and to highlight the Democratic party's concern with the issue by assembling the proposals under a package banner.

As described by DiOrio, the CAPTA had been created and developed independently of Assemblyman Vicencia's solicitations, with the bill's drafting coincident to the assembling of the Democratic package. The package, as noted by the sponsors, was both advantageous and somewhat worrisome. The publicity and support it generated around the issue of child abuse was propitious. Yet AB 2443 might become less visible in the midst of twenty-eight other bills. Subsequently, DiOrio and the sponsors set out to develop a campaign that would establish AB 2443 as markedly unique and significant.

Indeed, AB 2443 was singular in its approach. It was one of only a few bills that focused on prevention and unique in its emphasis on child education and an assertive response to abuse. It was also remarkably comprehensive, as its programs would potentially be available to all public school children in California at various stages throughout their educational careers. The bill campaign was to capitalize on these issues: California could fight child abuse by arming its children to stave off and report assault. The proposal offered an intriguing alternative to difficult, long-term programs aimed at the rehabilitation of adult abusers. With the children lay hope. The legislators just had to be convinced of it. To that end, the author and sponsors focused on tactics to persuade policymakers that their model of prevention training was effective and cost-efficient and that it carried substantial community support.

Bills originating from the assembly are first heard before relevant assembly committees. After passing each committee, the bill is brought for a vote before the entire assembly. If passed, the process is repeated in the senate. Finally, the legislation is carried to the governor for signing or veto.

The committees before which a bill is to be heard are formally selected by a Rules Committee on advice from a bill coordinator. The bill coordinator recommends committees that cover concerns relevant to the content or impact of a bill. The Rules Committee will generally confirm the coordinator's recommendations. Prior to committee selection, the bill author's legislative assistant may consult and negotiate with the bill coordinator, a procedure Stan DiOrio followed. It was determined that AB 2443 would be heard before the Criminal Law and Public Safety Committee (Byron Sher, chair); the Ways and Means

Committee (John Vasconcellos, chair, and of which Assemblywoman Waters was a member); and the Human Services Committee (Tom Bates, chair).

With the assembly committees settled, informational materials on AB 2443 were developed by Kain and Snowden in line with the anticipated concerns of the committee members and the legislators at large. The CAPTA would be promoted as a crime prevention measure, a bill that paid for itself by saving criminal investigation costs, and a tried and proven program boasting numerous and dramatic success stories. In line with this approach, advocates generated a continuous stream of bill flyers and announcements for distribution to the legislators. The flyers were catchy and easy to read. They presented the program as a two-pronged crime fighter. By instructing children in how to report abuse, the training curtailed ongoing crimes such as kidnapping and molestation. In addition, by reducing incidents of abuse, the program prevented future crimes often attributable to grown victims of child abuse.

The program also was displayed as a money saver. Child abuse is costly in society. The public pays a considerable sum to provide mental health and social services for abuse victims and to cover the cirminal investigation expenses incurred in pursuing and prosecuting offenders. The cost of prevention, estimated by the sponsors at $7 per child, was compared to the $400,000 police and court cost of the Tara Burke kidnapping case. Program advocates pointed out that the prevention of just one kidnapping in a county could pay for the entire cost of a prevention program within that county (depending on its size).

In addition to the flyers, several anecdotal CAPP success stories were compiled in a report titled "A Time for Hope."[4] The report provided examples of children who had escaped possible assault by utilizing assertiveness or self-defense methods learned through CAPP training. For example, using skills she had learned in a prevention workshop, a young girl named Trina was described as able to break away from a man who was dragging her to his car, and a brother and sister team employed a CAPP yell and physical maneuvers to fend off two teenage attackers. Also included in "A Time for Hope" were letters from children expressing their enthusiasm for CAPP training, as well as the results of an assessment of a CAPP program operating in a local school district in which children, parents, and teachers responded positively to questions asking their opinion of CAPP training.

Information supplied through written materials was supplemented by personal testimony. Witnesses before committee hearings included a carefully chosen mix of law enforcement personnel, professional child advocates, and parents of victims of kidnapping or assault. Witnesses often carried impressive credentials. For example, testifiers before the Ways and Means Committee included Richard Hesselroth, police inspector in the Tara Burke and Kevin Collins cases; Brooke Allison, former director of the Children's Bureau; and Kee MacFarland, a former staff member of the Federal National Center on Child Abuse and Neglect and a recognized expert in the identification and treatment of sexual abuse. Although children were ineligible to testify, child assault victims did sit before committees as adult witnesses graphically described their observances of the pain and suffering resulting from incidents of abuse. They implored legislators to support programs such as CAPP training. In addition, policymakers were addressed by Assemblywoman Waters, who spoke persuasively in support of a program model that taught children they had "the right not to be beaten, abused, or touched in an inappropriate place." As such, she pressed the legislature to recognize the unique and far-reaching potential of a program that focused on the education of children in the assertive handling of abuse.

Rich Snowden described the lobbying efforts on behalf of AB 2443 as "relentless."[5] In addition to generating a steady stream of written materials and striking dramatic personal testimony, the sponsors doggedly pursued legislators with phone calls and visits. The network of CAPP program organizers, always alert to the bill's progress, continued their vociferous endorsements, and Gloviell Rowland maintained an unflagging presence. Meanwhile, letters and calls from constituents kept pouring in. Even children were dialing their legislators' offices to register support for child abuse prevention. At the same time, the media began to give increasing coverage to the bill. Supporters had systematically contacted editorial writers at every major newspaper in California. As a result, pro–AB 2443 editorials were regularly appearing in newspapers across the state.

Intense lobbying efforts in the legislature were accompanied by an early approach to the governor's office. The largely Democratic legislature had not been expected to be antagonistic toward child abuse prevention legislation; Republican governor George Deukmejian was a question mark. While the bill was still before the legislature, Stan DiOrio set up a meeting with Maureen Higgins, deputy legislative secretary to the governor. Higgins was well aware of the bill via the media attention it was receiving and the large volume of pro–AB 2443 letters arriving at the governor's office.

In their presentation to her, supporters outlined and argued the specifics of the program proposed by the bill. They relayed success stories from "A Time for Hope," gave a CAPP curriculum demonstration, and detailed the program's statewide experience with operations in thirty locales. They were accompanied to the meetings by a parent of a victim of child abuse who described the abusive incident and made a plea for prevention efforts. The sponsors carried to the meeting a pamphlet that had been authorized by the governor several years before when he was attorney general. The pamphlet discussed mandatory reporting legislation that the then attorney general had sponsored and asserted the importance of child abuse crime prevention efforts. The AB 2443 sponsors then outlined the long-term crime prevention benefits of their proposed program. It appeared that the governor's deputy secretary had been favorably impressed.

A Timely but Tragic Boost

Political strategies aside, passage of AB 2443 was greatly aided by the emergence of a major child abuse case in southern California. Shrewd and diligent organizational work coupled with a timely but tragic boost from the McMartin case carried the bill to near unanimous passage in the legislature. In February 1984, just one month after AB 2443 was formally introduced, the McMartin Preschool case broke. Virginia and Raymond McMartin, day-care providers in the town of Manhattan Beach, California, were charged with physically, sexually, and emotionally abusing dozens of preschool children over several years. The story shocked the public and state legislators and exploded in the media. The McMartin School had been licensed by the state. Constituents were demanding an explanation and corrective action.

As the case developed and unfolded, legislators were pressed to respond. The public wanted something done, and AB 2443 provided a clear opportunity for action. As Stan DiOrio noted, the publicity "cleared the road to passage."[6] The bill boasted a strong, influential author, a vociferous, enthusiastic grassroots constituency, and a fitting plan for the systematic implementation of a statewide, state-administered prevention training program directed at children in preschool through high school. The bill had been intensively lobbied and persuasively argued. Hard organizational efforts had been effective. It moved without much difficulty through the assembly's Crime and Public Safety, Ways and Means, and Human Services committees. Its passage in the assembly virtually ensured the same in the senate. The bill was heard without argument before the senate's Finance and Judiciary committees, passing the full senate with a unanimous vote of 40 to 0. The issue of child abuse was politically uncontestable. The bill campaign for the prevention training model had been exceedingly well organized, with the proposed program perceived by the policymakers as effective and appropriate.

Having passed the assembly and senate, AB 2443 went to the governor's desk. Impressed with the early presentation by the bill's sponsor and advocates, Maureen Higgins had given the governor a favorable recommendation on the bill. As described by Higgins, the governor found the bill well written and voiced approval of its unambiguous construction, detailed program outline, and explicit funding guidelines. The project appeared to be cost-effective and a solid crime prevention effort. In addition, child abuse was a hot topic politically. The governor signed the bill for its full appropriation.

Points of Debate: Refining the Bill

Although issue was taken with various technical aspects of the bill, few persons made claim against its philosophical or programmatic premise. Many of the more significant technical problems with the bill were brought to the fore early in the legislative process and negotiated with swift and flexible response from the author and sponsors. As former OCAP director Bruce Kennedy observed, the general political reaction to the initial draft of the bill could be summarized as "a good program that cost too much and contained flaws that made it difficult to administer."[7] Early in the process, it was clear that for the bill to move along, the program cost would have to be cut from the proposed figure of $22 million annually. Subsequently, the authors and sponsors knocked the price down to $11,235,000 over eighteen months, a figure they quoted as based on the statement by advocates that prevention programming could be provided at a cost of $7 per child.

In addition to cost, there were concerns about having prevention training programs required by state law. Very early in the legislative process, the California School Board Association informed Stan DiOrio that they would fight a mandated program. School administrators feared objections from conservative communities over instruction that made references to sexual abuse. If the program was mandated, the association wanted individual school districts to be given the authority to screen the content of prevention training curricula. A compromise was reached. The state mandate was dropped, and the programs were made voluntary. Individual school districts could choose whether or not to participate in the prevention training program specified by the legislation.

Meanwhile, some debate had arisen among policymakers as to whether the bill should be administered by the Education Department as opposed to OCAP. Here again, educational professionals took issue. The Education Department viewed the program as an administrative burden that could overload the staff. Many teachers had written legislators to voice concern that they not be required to serve as workshop instructors; they felt the AB 2443 program should be handled by outside program organizers. With educational administrators and staff opposed to a school-administered project, AB 2443 was destined to be housed within OCAP.

Some questions were raised about the training curriculum specified in the legislation. Several non-CAPP child abuse prevention models were extant in the state, including the Children's Self-Help Project, Illusion Theatre, and others. Many of the programs were similar conceptually to CAPP but different in detail. The staffs of these programs worried that the curriculum guidelines specified by the bill might be so narrowly CAPP-oriented as to exclude other programs from funding. Organized by Pnina Tobin of the Children's Self-Help Project in San Francisco, these program practitioners made contact with the author, legislators, and OCAP personnel to voice their insistence that their projects not be excluded. Although bearing a distinct CAPP stamp, the legislative language was in fact written broadly enough to include conceptually similar models. As first drafted, AB 2443 was intended to fund private, nonprofit grassroots organizations. On this point Assemblywoman Waters was adamant; she did not want a program that would finance established public/bureaucratic programs. After much wrangling a compromise was reached; public programs could apply for funding but would receive low priority in allocation considerations.

As the bill made its way through the assembly and senate committees and was reviewed by offices such as the Finance Department, the Department of Social Services, and OCAP, several other technical adjustments were suggested to effect a smoother implementation. Among these were amendments to the timing of appropriation, revision of the portion of funding allocated to state administration, and correcting logistical problems. These technical changes were collectively addressed and implemented in a clean-up amendment to the bill, AB 147. The amendment was signed into law on June 25, 1985, and the CAPTA was officially implemented in July 1985.

Conceptual Accord

Interestingly, dispute over technical issues was not accompanied by a wide-ranging debate over the concept and value of the proposed prevention training program. As the bill was heard before committees in the assembly and senate, legislators repeatedly posed the question "Does the program work?" Each in turn signified satisfaction with the answers supplied by the author and sponsors: Anecdotal evidence indicated that children participating in CAPP training learned techniques that increased the likelihood of disclosure and fending off of assault,[7] thus decreasing the likelihood of abuse. The legislators did not press for empirical data on the program's effectiveness. Written materials on the program prepared by the sponsors suggested that it was difficult to quantitatively measure the phenomena that had been prevented. The training, it was argued, had some positive effect, whether scientifically documented or not; that was enough to make it amenable. The legislators did not request or pursue evaluations of other extant prevention models. The author and sponsors described CAPP as the most widely used child-oriented prevention model in the state. The language of the bill was written to include this and conceptually similar training methods. The legislators were satisfied that the proposed model was as apt as any in operation.

The program's experience was particularly persuasive. CAPP programs were already operating in thirty locales throughout the state. According to the sponsors, this demonstrated the project as tried administratively and tested pragmatically. Indeed, a state-funded pilot of the program was not discussed much by legislators, as the attention given child abuse in the media and among the public seemed to warrant prompt action. Politically, the time was right for the immediate implementation of a statewide prevention program. AB 2443 stood as a solid response to a pressing issue. A pilot program was viewed as a code for delay. Delay could signify that policymakers were not wholeheartedly committed to preventing child abuse. The media furor and seeming urgency of the problem also may have precluded debate of other potentially controversial elements of the proposed legislation. Due to the McMartin case, the inclusion of preschoolers in the program was accepted without question. Issues such as the possible complications of false reports, adverse parental or child response to the workshop material, the ability of program instructors to respond adequately to disclosure, the relationship between the Department of Social Services and the training programs, and the specific content of the curriculum did not emerge as topics of much discussion or concern. Legislators were under pressure to do something about child abuse. AB 2443 had been convincingly presented as a visible, community-sanctioned, and effective plan of action.

Evaluation and Evolution

The CAPTA was written to include program monitoring and evaluation. As noted by Assemblywoman Waters, "AB 2443 was constructed and pursued as a means by which life could be made safer for children. With its implementation, our responsibility is now to gather data on the program to see specifically what is working and how it works. We expect to modify and refine the project in a strengthening of our prevention efforts."[8] As a landmark effort in prevention programming, the CAPTA is expected to evolve. Moved by an influential author and a committed, well-organized child advocacy constituency and developed in the midst of intense public concern over the issue, AB 2443 was embraced by the legislature with much hope and enthusiasm. Now that the dust has settled, the funding has been secured, and the program is in place, a number of questions arise regarding its methods and its impact in the area of child abuse prevention. The study reported in the following chapters was designed to explore these questions and advance the understanding of child abuse prevention programs in California and nationwide.

Notes

1. Most of the information on the development of this bill was obtained through interviews with key actors in the legislative process. These interviews were conducted by Allison Zippay between June and September 1986 with the following subjects: Kate Kain, CAP Training Center of Northern California; Rich Snowden, CAP Training Center of Northern California; Stan DiOrio, legislative assistant to Assemblywoman Maxine Waters; Assemblywoman Maxine Waters; Maureen Higgins, deputy legislative secretary to Governor Deukmejian; Bob Green, OCAP; Linda Reese, OCAP; Bruce Kennedy, former director, OCAP; Catherine Camp, former legislative analyst to the Assembly Human Services Committee; Jane Callahan, legislative chair, California Consortium of Child Abuse Councils; Kathy Baxter-Stern, San Francisco Child Abuse Council;

Gloviell Rowland, Southern California Child Abuse Prevention Training Center; Pnina Tobin, Children's Self-Help Project; Chet Olsen, consultant to the Assembly Select Committee on Child Abuse; Linda Vooris, Commission on the Status of Women.

2. California Department of Social Services, Statistical Services Branch.

3. Maxine Waters, Personal Communication. Summer, 1986.

4. "A Time for Hope." Report prepared by the Child Assault Prevention Training Center of Northern California, Berkeley, 1984.

5. Rich Snowden, Personal Communication. Summer, 1986.

6. Stan DiOrio, Personal Communication. Summer, 1986.

7. Bruce Kennedy, Personal Communication. Summer, 1986.

8. Maxine Waters, Personal Communication. Summer, 1986.

2
Preschool Prevention in California: Programs and Curricula

C hild abuse primary prevention programs such as the ones mandated in California are still in a fledgling state. Little is known about their effect on the young children who participate in them. While some anecdotal evidence exists regarding the various consequences of these approaches to primary prevention, there are several important issues surrounding early educational efforts on which little systematic analysis of empirical evidence is available, particularly for preschool programs. These issues concern the most useful substantive content for educational models, the most effective instructional techniques for preschool children, and the impact of these preventive programs on children, parents, preschools, and local protective service agencies.

Many of the questions surrounding the impact of these programs ultimately relate to the design of their substantive content and instructional techniques. There is little agreement on the most effective content and instructional techniques for preschool programs. One of the major concerns in this area regards the appropriateness of making children, often very young children, responsible for discerning between good touch and bad touch or expecting them to know when appropriate signs of affection become inappropriate acts of abuse. It is unclear how well three- to five-year-old children can absorb these lessons.

The impact of these programs on preschool personnel also is highly uncertain. There is impressionistic evidence that the fear of being charged with actual or attempted sexual abuse has led some providers to close down their daycare facilities or to be more restrained in the level of affection shown to the children in their charge. Another source of anxiety among preschool personnel involves their legal responsibility for reporting the self-disclosed cases of abuse, which are likely to increase as programs heighten sensitivity to these acts and children's rights to protection.

The magnitude and diversity of materials designed to conduct sexual abuse prevention programs for preschool children under AB 2443 offer a unique opportunity for an empirical assessment of educational approaches to this primary prevention strategy. Addressing the issues noted above, this study examines the impact of child abuse prevention training in the context of the following questions:

How do these educational programs affect the children's perceptions of appropriate expressions of affection, responses to uncertain or threatening situations, and ability to protect themselves from harm? What do children learn?

How do parents perceive and evaluate the effect of these programs? What do parents learn from their participation in the programs?

How do these programs affect the school systems in which they are conducted? How do teachers respond to prevention training?

How well does the curricula content reflect the cognitive development of preschool children?

What are the normative implications of the curricula content?

Programs

Seven prevention projects were selected for participation in this evaluation. The projects were chosen for inclusion in the sample based on their stated program goals, geographic location, community composition (socioeconomic and cultural), and auspices (community or school based). A final prerequisite for selection was the projects' ability to meet our criteria for participation, including securing school sites, scheduling workshops when requested, and participating in a lengthy site visit and interview.

The seven projects that participated in the study are described briefly below:

Child Assault Prevention Project (CAPP), Oakland

The Child Assault Prevention (CAP) Training Center of Northern California has a regional program and a local program. Its regional program serves as the training center for the AB 2443 projects in northern California and provides technical assistance to fifty-three child abuse prevention programs in forty-eight counties. Its local program provides the CAPP curriculum to schools in northern Alameda County.

The training center and CAPP programs are based on a feminist rape prevention theory. This perspective stresses the importance of developing co-responsibility among all community members for stopping violence against women and children. Rape prevention programs focus on four major goals: to build women's strength, to extend women's mobility, to promote women's independence, and to guarantee women's freedom. The CAPP program extends these goals to child assault prevention. The goals of the CAPP program are to make child sexual assault a public issue; to change the social position of children as powerless; and to reduce children's isolation in the community.

The CAPP elementary school curriculum was originally designed in the mid-1970s by Women Against Rape of Columbus, Ohio. The curriculum was widely disseminated across the United States and was introduced to the training center in 1981. In 1982 the training center developed the curriculum to be used specifically with preschool children. Visual aids are used for the children's curriculum. These include pictures of children feeling safe, strong, and free and child-size dolls that participate in the children's role playing with workshop leaders.

The children's curriculum is provided by two members of the CAPP staff. One person acts as the main facilitator, while the other person assists in the role playing. The curriculum is presented on three consecutive days for twenty to thirty minutes each day. CAPP staff prefer to have groups of ten children but will include up to fifteen children if necessary. Children are not separated by age, so those between two and one-half and five years of age may be represented in each group.

Children's Self-Help Project (CSHP), San Francisco

In 1980 a group of professionals involved in child sexual abuse treatment gathered together to discuss the need for prevention. The San Francisco Child Abuse Council was formed and received funding for training with the Illusion Theater (Minneapolis) and CAPP (Women Against Rape, Columbus, Ohio). From the training, an elementary school prevention curriculum was developed and a pilot project was sponsored in 1981 for eighty San Francisco children.

CSHP focuses solely on prevention but provides a variety of community services beyond training for children. The project staff believe that children can be empowered to protect themselves and that they can lessen their vulnerability to abuse. Workshops in primary prevention are available to children ages two and one half to fifteen years, as well as to their parents and teachers.

At the center of the children's curriculum are the beliefs that sexual abuse is a manifestation of a power imbalance between adults and children; children have intuitive power; children deserve our respect; children have the right to a safe childhood, free from abuse; and sexual abuse is never the child's fault. The format for the preschool curriculum is similar to that for the elementary school child, but the language is simpler and there is more repetition with preschoolers. Songs are used throughout the presentation to help reinforce concepts and encourage children's involvement.

The CSHP curriculum is presented by two staff members plus one volunteer (observer/facilitator). The workshop lasts approximately one-half hour and is presented on two consecutive days. The curriculum is designed for children ages two and one-half to five years and can be presented either in mixed or single age groups. Instructors use child-size puppets to develop a nonthreatening rapport with the children.

Touch Safety Program (TSP), San Rafael

In 1978 the San Francisco Foundation provided funding to launch the Marin Child Sexual Abuse Treatment Program. This grant was supplemented with an in-kind match from the County of Marin. Part of this program included a prevention component known as the Touch Safety Program. The TSP is operated out of the county's Department of Social Services office, which facilitates the program's relationship with that county's children's protective services component. The project's goals are to reduce children's vulnerability to abuse and to prevent child abuse. The first curriculum was written for elementary school children.

In 1983 the preschool curriculum was developed in response to community interest. The curriculum relies on numerous visual aids. Animal puppets are used to personify and present the concepts, and red, yellow, and green light faces are used to illustrate the Touch Continuum.

Project staff lead the children's workshops, which consist of three sessions presented within one week. Each presentation takes between twenty and thirty minutes; group size is limited to ten children.

Talking About Touching (TAT), Palo Alto

The Child Advocacy Council began in 1979 as the Mid-Peninsula Child Advocacy Council and merged with the Santa Clara County Child Abuse Council in 1982 to become the current organization.

The curricula used by the Child Advocacy Council are *Talking About Touching II* (preschool curriculum), *Talking About Touching* (for grades K through 5), and *Personal Safety and Decision Making* (all designed by the Committee for Children, Seattle, Washington). The central goals of all curricula include the child's right to say no, the concept of body ownership, and the importance of telling someone about an abusive incident.

In selecting a curriculum to present to children, the Child Advocacy Council staff sought input from the director of the San Mateo Department of Social Services and the superintendent of schools. The Committee for Children curricula were chosen with an eye to teacher participation in the program. Agency staff believed this approach might be more cost-efficient and might provide children greater continuity with their regular school program.

The preschool curriculum consists of twenty-seven lessons, each one about fifteen to twenty minutes long. The curriculum is presented in a three- to six-week period with three to five lessons per week. The lessons are intended for children between the ages of three and five years. Each lesson consists of a black-and-white drawing on one side of a card, with the teacher's instructions and a story on the other side. The teacher reads the brief story, then uses the questions as a discussion guide to ensure the children's comprehension of the material. The program includes concepts such as bike safety, traffic safety, use of matches, and electrical outlets. It includes not only the prevention of sexual abuse, but the prevention of physical abuse as well.

Child Abuse Prevention, Intervention and Education (CAPIE), San Bernardino

The CAPIE program is housed in the Family Service Agency (FSA) of San Bernardino. That agency's primary goals are to contribute to harmonious family interrelationships; they believe in strengthening positive values of family life and in promoting healthy personality development. In addition to their work in child abuse prevention, the agency provides a variety of other services to the community in the form of counseling and family support.

CAPIE services are fairly recent additions to the agency. In 1984 the FSA received funding from the AB 2443 legislation to provide training and education to the community. The goal of the prevention project is to prevent child abuse and neglect. To accomplish this, the project works at reducing children's vulnerability by increasing the awareness and sensitivity of parents, school staff, and community members. The child abuse prevention curriculum for preschoolers is a compilation of several widely known curricula. Carol Plummer's *We Help Ourselves* and Marlys Olsen's *Personal Safety* are combined with activities and concepts designed by a local school district. The curriculum attempts to encourage the personal safety of the child while introducing age-appropriate facts about abuse.

The children's workshop is a one-day, fifteen- to twenty-minute presentation conducted by one staff member. Two other staff members observe the presentation and assist when the children's attention begins to drift. The curriculum is designed for children ages two to five years. A small hand puppet is used to help focus the children's attention, and a coloring page is left with the children to reinforce concepts.

Youth Safety Awareness Project (YSAP), Culver City

The Didi Hirsch Community Mental Health Center was incorporated in 1942 as a private, nonprofit agency to provide comprehensive mental health care to the community. The prevention program is housed within the center and serves a large portion of Los Angeles County. Their principal goal is to make organized groups aware of the prevalence and seriousness of sexual assault. Their hope is to promote preventive action, and to provide information on what to expect and how to cope with the crisis of sexual assault. The original curriculum, designed to help convey the concepts of sexual abuse to children, emerged out of a collaborative effort between Didi Hirsch and the Los Angeles Commission on Assaults Against Women in 1976.

The Didi Hirsch child abuse prevention curriculum for preschoolers is titled *Youth Safety Awareness Project*. The children's curriculum embraces some of the tenets of the rape crisis movement familiar in the CAPP models and broadens that perspective to a community education and community action approach (due to the community mental health influence). The program teaches children to take care of themselves with the added support of the family and community.

The children's workshop is a one-day, fifteen- to thirty-minute presentation conducted by one Didi Hirsch staff member. The curriculum is presented to preschool children ages two to five years.

Stop Abuse through Family Education (SAFE), El Cajon

The El Cajon Valley Unified School District's involvement in abuse prevention began in 1981 through a collaboration with Children's Hospital in San Diego. At that time Children's Hospital and the Cajon Valley Unified School District, with the help of a grant from the National Center on Child Abuse and Neglect, worked together to develop a safety curriculum called the STOP program.

With the receipt of AB 2443 monies in December 1985, the school district revised the STOP program, turning it into Project SAFE, the curriculum currently used. Project SAFE's goals are to increase the awareness of school staff, parents, and children about the issue of child abuse; to provide children with the knowledge they need to prevent abuse and to get help; and to create ties between the community and the school district. The staff at Project SAFE feel that it is important to involve the schools actively in the prevention project and to be able to leave the schools with some type of prevention program if and when state funding is discontinued.

The curriculum stresses the importance of adult responsibility in maintaining children's safety. The children's workshop is a one-day, thirty-minute presentation. It is conducted in the children's classroom by two staff members.

These seven prevention programs each selected a preschool in their service area to be included in the evaluation. The preschool sites ranged from urban to semirural locations. Their size and the socioeconomic status of the families involved were equally diverse, as table 2–1 shows.

Prevention Curricula for Children

Written children's curricula were available for five of the seven projects studied: Child Assault Prevention Project (CAPP), Children's Self-Help Project (CSHP), Talking About Touching (TAT), Touch Safety Program (TSP), and Project SAFE. The discussion of the dominant prevention concepts presented in the following pages is based primarily on definitions from these written materials.[1] Two of the projects did not have written curricula at the time of

Table 2–1
Preschool Sites

	A	B	C	D	E	F	G
Community setting	Urban	Urban	Suburban	Suburban	Semirural	Urban	Suburban
Number of children	168	35	100	57	45	100	50
Teacher: child ratio	1:8	1:5	1:12	1:12	1:7	1:8	1:8
Parent participation	No	Yes	No	No	Yes	Yes	Yes
Years in operation	75	40	10	15	18		3
Ethnic composition	80% B* 16% A* 4% H*	58% W* 3% B 30% A 9% H	90% W 4% B 4% A	80% W 10% A 10% H	25% W 33% B 40% H 2% O*	60% B 40% H	75% W 20% H 5% O
Educational setting	Day care	Preschool	Preschool	Day care	Preschool	Day care	Preschool
Funding	State funded	Private	Private	State and private	State funded	State funded	State funded

*B = black; A = Asian; H = Hispanic; W = white; o = other

Table 2–2
Curricula Concepts

Concepts	CAPP*—Site A	CSHP*—Site B	TSP*—Site C
Good touch	Touches that don't hurt.	"Heart Touch"—That's a touch that feels good and safe. It's a touch that both people like and both people want.	"Green Light Touch" makes us feel happy and we want it to go on and on.
Confusing touch		"Question Mark (?) Touch"—A "?" touch is a mixed-up touch. It's kind of confusing. You may want it at first but then change your mind. Or you may like the person who is doing the touching but you may not like how the touch feels.	"Yellow Light Touch" makes us feel mixed-up . . . maybe happy and then mad. When we get a yellow light touch we can say *stop* and take a *time out* and if that doesn't work you can *tell*.
Bad touch		"No Touch"—You do not like this kind of touch. You want a "no" touch to stop.	"Red Light Touch" makes us feel bad and to a red light touch we say *stop*.
Verbal assertiveness	You want to run away. And you want to tell someone about what happened.	Say no and tell. Say stop. Tell someone else. (If necessary tell the same person again.)	Say no Ready to go Yell Yell
Private parts	Breasts, penis, vagina	The mouth, the chest, between the legs, and the bottom.	. . . the parts you cover with your underwear. The names for the private parts are penis, vagina, and anus. Private means that these are special parts of your body that are all yours, they don't belong to anyone else.

TAT*—Site D	CAPIE*—Site E	YSAP*—Site F	SAFE*—Site G
. . . makes you feel good.	Touches that don't hurt.	"OK touch"—A touch that feels good to you.	Most of the touches you get are good kinds of touches, like when you get hugs, kisses, or when you get a pat on the back.
Makes you feel "mixed-up" or "icky." It's one that's fun at the beginning but ends up hurting. You like the person but not the touch. Someone you don't want to, touches you.	"Uh-oh Touch"— When you're not sure if it's good or bad.	(only used for ages four and up and then only at presenter's discretion) A touch that starts feeling comfortable and fun then goes too far and you might want it to stop.	There's a touch on your private parts that's not okay. When an older or bigger person wants to touch you in your private place, when you don't need any help, that's not okay. Sometimes an older person may want to rub or lick or kiss a kid in their private parts, and this is not okay.
One that hurts.	Something that hurts us.	A touch that feels bad inside. Or a touch that makes you feel yucky inside. Or a touch that does not feel okay.	Some touches do not feel good and are not okay.
Anytime you feel un-comfortable, "Icky," or mixed-up about a touch, tell someone you trust about how you are feeling.	Stand up, chin up, shoulder raised, fist clenched, look mean. Say no.	If you're not comfor-table with a touch, you can do some-thing about it. Say no. Walk or run away. Just think of words that mean "stop" to you.	Stop it! Get away! Tell, tell, tell!
Private body parts. Parts covered by bathing suit.	Parts covered by bathing suit. You don't have to share with anybody.	(Only talk about this with older kids, or if the children bring it up themselves) Parts of the body their bathing suit covers. Special parts of your body you need to keep safe.	Private parts are the parts between your legs covered by your underwear. Private parts have openings that you use to go to the bathroom.

Table 2–2 *continued*

Concepts	CAPP*—Site A	CSHP*—Site B	TSP*—Site C
Body rights	All the parts of your body have the right to be safe, strong, and free.	Your body is your own special property.	Every one of you has your very own body.
Perpetrator		It can be a woman, a man, older people, younger people, people who wear uniforms, people who wear suits, strangers, and people you know (baby-sitter, uncle, father).	. . . it might be a stranger or it might be someone you know . . . someone in your family, someone your parents know well, or your teacher, your friend, or a baby-sitter.
Guilt/blame		If a child is touched in private parts and doesn't want to be, it's always the fault of the person who's touching the child or asking the child to touch him or her.	It's not your fault if you get a private parts touch.
Okay private parts touches			—The doctor gives you a shot in the bottom.—You get hurt there, and Mom and Dad use a medicine.—Your mom and dad diaper the baby.—Is it OK for you to touch yourself in your private parts? (Yes, in private)
Self-defense yell	It is very ferocious and it means two things. It means I am strong so don't mess with me, and it means I need help.	It's a yell that will help to keep you safe.	If you get a red light feeling, you can yell from deep in your belly.

TAT*—Site D	CAPIE*—Site E	YSAP*—Site F	SAFE*—Site G
Your body is your own.		Your body is special because it belongs to you and nobody else.	. . . you can learn to take good care of your body and keep yourself safe. Say this with me: "My body is mine! I have the right to be safe! My body's mine from my toes to my top. So leave me alone when you hear me say stop!"
(Cited examples in stories) Stranger, baby-sitter, friend of parent.	Peer—a friend of yours. A grown-up person that you know or your family knows.	Stranger.	
If someone older does touch your private body parts you are not bad.		It's not the child's fault	
Changing diapers, wiping bottoms, doctor—for health, getting a bath, touching self.	You can (touch your private parts) . . . a doctor, a nurse . . . Mom and Dad when you are sick.		

Table 2–2 *continued*

Concepts	CAPP*—Site A	CSHP*—Site B	TSP*—Site C
Safety space	Stand more than an arm's distance from someone you don't know.	Keep an arm's distance.	A safety space is as big as a broomstick. If you keep that space from a stranger, you will stay safe.
Safe	Safe is when you know everything.	Feeling safe feels warm inside and out. Feeling safe feels like no one can hurt you.	Taking care of your body.

*CAPP = Child Assault Prevention Project; CSHP = Children's Self-Help Project; TSP = Touch Safety Program; TAT = Talking about Touching; CAPIE = Child Abuse Prevention,

the study: the Child Abuse Prevention, Intervention and Education (CAPIE) Project and the Youth Safety Awareness Project (YSAP). Descriptions of these projects were obtained through observation of the children's workshop and discussions with project staff. In this section we discuss some of the concepts presented in the curricula and point out the similarities and differences in the way the projects present them. (See table 2–2.)

Touch Continuum

The concept of a Touch Continuum is central to most programs; only CAPP does not utilize it. The curricula differentiate touches by the affective or physical reaction the recipient experiences, categorizing them generally as good, confusing, and bad or safe and unsafe. The actual labels and terminology differ among projects. CSHP uses symbolic terms ("Heart Touches," "Question Mark Touches," and "No Touches"), TSP offers a familiar visual image ("Green Light Touches," "Yellow Light Touches," and "Red Light Touches"), and TAT refers to safe and unsafe touches. CAPIE only labels the confusing touch ("Uh-oh" Touch) and describes the other two in general terms. YSAP and SAFE discuss the different types of touches but do not define them by name.

Positive touches (hugs, kisses, pats) and their affective component ("Safe touches are caring touches";[2] ". . . a touch both people like and both people want"[3]) are fairly straightforward. Negative touching is defined thus: "A red light touch makes us feel sad or mad . . . what can we say to a red light touch? Stop!"[4] "Unsafe touches . . . which hurt our bodies or our feelings."[5]

The middle, or confusing, touch does not share this clarity. Most projects offer a dual definition: "A '?' touch is a mixed up touch. It's kind of confusing. You may want it at first but then change your mind. Or you may like the person

TAT*—Site D	CAPIE*—Site E	YSAP*—Site F	SAFE*—Site G
			Taking care of your body.

Intervention and Education; YSAP = Youth Safety Awareness Project; SAFE = Stop Abuse through Family Education

who's doing the touching but you may not like how the touch feels."[6] "Safe touches don't hurt or scare us. Confusing touches start out being safe and then don't seem safe after awhile. Confusing touches make us feel mixed up or scared."[7]

SAFE eschews the complex definitions cited above and offers a description of specific situations that could be considered confusing:

> When an older or bigger person wants to touch you in your private place when you don't need any help, that's not okay. Sometimes an older person may want to rub or lick or kiss a kid in their private parts, or they want you to touch, lick or kiss them in their private parts, and this is not okay.[8]

Children's Rights

Also central to many programs is the concept of children's rights. The CAPP workshop focuses on the concept of empowering children. Workshop leaders encourage the children to strive toward self-assertion and to recognize their rights to be safe, strong, and free in all aspects of their lives.

Other programs refer to children's body rights, essentially their rights to avoid any harm that might befall them at the hands of bigger people. Body rights and verbal assertion are considered closely connected. SAFE has a brief poem that illustrates this point:

> My body is mine
> From my toes to my top.
> So leave me alone
> When you hear me say STOP!!![9]

TSP uses the tune "The Farmer in the Dell" to accompany its message:

> My body is my own
> Though I'm not fully grown
> I'm old enough to tell you so
> And I am saying "No!"[10]

Other projects encourage a sense of body rights more succinctly: "Your body is your own special property"[11] and "Your body is special because it belongs to you and nobody else."[12]

Concept of Being Safe

The concept of being or feeling safe is introduced directly in three of the curricula. CAPP says, "Safe is when you know everything is all right."[13] TSP states, "Safety means taking care of your body."[14] CSHP sees it as a sense of security: "Feeling safe feels warm inside and out. Feeling safe feels like no one can hurt you."[15]

Other programs that do not directly discuss being or feeling safe include the necessity for seeking or maintaining a sense of safety through assertive and protective measures. For example, TAT introduces its abuse prevention program with a discussion of general safety, then leads into the personal safety aspect of the program.

Secrets

Secrets and their ramifications are among the key concepts covered in most prevention curricula. In the TAT curriculum, the teacher asks the children to define secrets. The curriculum provides definitions for the teacher as well, including "When something is known, but is kept hidden from certain people."[16]

All the curricula focus on the dichotomy between good and bad secrets. Good secrets are those that fall into the category of surprises that "you keep for a little while, and after you tell, everyone has a good time."[17] Conversely, "a bad secret doesn't make you feel good."[18] CSHP tells children what they can do if they are touched and sworn to secrecy. "When someone says, 'don't tell anyone ever!' when they touch you in your private parts or want you to touch them, you can tell someone. You don't have to keep this kind of secret."[19]

The two concepts of bad touch and bad secret have been further intertwined by TSP:

> Secret touching is when someone bigger or older than you asks to touch your private parts, or you to touch theirs, and tells you to keep it a secret. . . .
>
> [S]ecrets like that make you feel "Uh-oh"—like private parts touching— those aren't OK.[20]

Guilt and Blame

In addition to all the frightening aspects of sexual abuse, many programs add a note of reassurance for the children by telling them that, no matter what the circumstances, the abused child is never at fault. For example, "If a grown-up touches your private body parts, you are not bad. It is not your fault. Remember, most grown-ups give caring, safe touches."[21]

The fault, guilt, or blame rests solely on the perpetrator who, as he or she is older than the child, should know better: "If a child can't stop a touch, is it the child's fault? No, it is never the child's fault. It's always the fault of the bigger or older person who's touching the child."[22]

Strangers

"Stranger danger" is an integral aspect of all the curricula, although some give this greater emphasis than others. Children are admonished not to talk to strangers without parental permission, not to take items from strangers, and not to go anywhere with strangers. The stranger is universally described as someone the child does not know. TAT uses a picture of a man and two children, with the following script: "Jason and Suzanne were playing in the park. A man came and offered to buy them some ice cream bars if they would go for a walk with him."[23] Subsequent questions probe for what the children might do to stay safe. TSP defines a stranger as "someone who does not live with you and your parents do not know well."[24]

Two projects, CAPP and TSP, include in their definitions the fact that strangers are not solely the stereotype of an evil appearing person:

> "Can a woman be someone you don't know? Can a baby be someone you don't know? . . . Can a stranger be fat? Can a stranger have this color skin? . . . A stranger can be anyone. It's just someone we don't know."[25]

> "A stranger can be nice or not nice. A stranger is a person; never someone in the movies or a monster. It can be a man or a woman."[26]

> "Most strangers are green light people."[27]

The concept that most strangers are safe people is unique to TSP.

Perpetrators

Identification of the perpetrator differs based on the philosophy of the program. CAPP, which emphasizes empowerment of children under all circumstances, does not label abuse per se but does discuss uncomfortable touches from an uncle. The familiar, and possibly trusted, person as perpetrator is approached by CSHP with the following statement: "It can be a woman, a man, older people, younger people, people who wear uniforms, people who wear suits, strangers and people you know."[28]

Further emphasis is given to this in role playing involving a baby-sitter, an uncle, and a father. Pictures and stories in the TAT curriculum include a stranger, a baby-sitter, and a friend of the child's parents as possible perpetrators. TSP informs the children that a perpetrator "could be a stranger or someone you know. . . . What is someone you know? Someone in your family, someone your parents know well, or your teacher."[29] CAPIE emphasizes the stranger as perpetrator, while SAFE emphasizes the familiar person.

Private Parts

There is a lack of consensus regarding how to label the private parts of the body. Some projects avoid anatomical terminology, preferring to refer to the private parts indirectly, for example: "The bathing suit covers up the private parts of [the] body"[30]; "[those] which you don't have to share with anybody"[31]; and "[the] special parts of your body you need to keep safe."[32]

Three projects are more specific: "breasts, penis, vagina"[33]; "the mouth, the chest, between the legs and the bottom"[34]; and "Private parts are the parts between your legs covered by your underwear. Private parts have openings that you use to go to the bathroom."[35]

TSP offers a more detailed definition, covering both approaches: "the parts you cover with your bathing suit or underwear. The names for the private parts are penis, vagina and anus. Private means that these are special parts of your body that are all yours, they don't belong to anyone else."[36]

One of the aims of abuse prevention programs is to teach the children that their private parts are exactly what the term implies, private. Several programs (CAPIE, TAT, TSP) amend the message, however, with an explanation that there are times when it is important that someone else touch the child's genitals or chest. Instances when touching is considered appropriate are those involving health or hygiene.

Safety Space

In teaching defense skills, three of the programs instruct the children to keep a specifically defined distance from strangers. For example, "there is a special way that you should stand if you meet someone you don't know. Stick out your arm. You should stand more than this far away from someone you don't know."[37] This distance also is recommended by CSHP. TSP refers to "a safety space [which] is as big as a broomstick. . . . If you keep that space from a stranger, you will stay safe."[38]

Verbal Assertiveness

All the projects tell the children that, should someone try to harm them, they have the right to say no firmly and to tell someone they trust about the episode, for example: "You can say 'No!', push the person's hand away, run away, and tell."[39] Similarly, CAPP says: "You want to run away. And you want to tell someone about what happened. It is very important to tell someone."[40] CSHP encourages repetition when needed: "You know, sometimes the first person a child tells doesn't believe them. That's why it's important to tell, and tell, and tell, until someone does believe you."[41]

Jingles are also popular:

Say No
Ready to Go
Yell
Tell.[42]

Stand up, chin up,
shoulders raised,
fist clenched,
look mean,
Say NO![43]

Stop it! Get away! Tell! Tell![44]

TSP brings in parental roles and the potential support that should come from them: "What have your parents told you to say to a stranger who asks you to go along (with him/her)? . . . You can say: I have to go ask my parents."[45]

Self-Defense Yell

Three of the projects carry assertiveness beyond firmly saying no and teach the children a self-defense yell, emanating from the diaphragm. They explain that since this sound is unlike any usual yell, it will attract attention and help when used (and if not misused). It is considered "a yell that will help to keep you safe."[46] According to CAPP, it has a dual meaning: "It is very ferocious and means two things. It means I am strong so don't mess with me, and it means I need help."[47]

Physical Self-Defense

In addition to the self-defense yell, CAPP also teaches children to fight back if they are grabbed by an assailant. The children are advised: "You can stomp on their foot (demonstrate stomp). And you can bite, scratch, punch—you can do anything you can to get away."[48]

Table 2–3
Parent Curricula

Parent Meetings	CAPP*	CSHP*	TSP*
Conducted by	CAPP paid staff	Two CSHP staff (one paid, one volunteer)	One TSP paid staff
Duration of Meeting	Two to three hours combined with teacher workshop	Two hours	One to two
Proximity to Children's Workshop	One to two weeks before	One week before	One week before
Content of Parent Meetings: Goal of the children's curriculum as presented to parents	To make child sexual assault a public issue; to change the social position of children as powerless; to reduce children's isolation in the community	To teach children to protect themselves because we can't be with them twenty-four hours a day	Not specified
Overview of the Problem	Discussion of myths, statistics, and dynamics.	One in three girls and one in seven boys are abused before age eighteen	Discussion of myths and realities of child abuse
Definition of Children's Rights	Right to be safe, strong, and free	Right to a safe childhood, free from abuse	Not specified
Skills Taught to Children	Kick, stomp on the instep, elbow to the groin or chin, bite, hit, scream, anything to get away. Self-defense yell	Keep an arm's distance, say no, run, self-defense yell	Say no, run, tell
What To Do If Child Discloses	Gives names of referrals and resources	Support child Believe child Call resources	Not specified

TAT*	YSAP*	CAPIE*	SAFE*
One TAT paid staff	One or two paid staff	Three paid CAPIE staff	One paid SAFE staff
One and one-half hours	One hour	One and one-half hours	One hour
Flexible—within the month	One week before	One week to several months before	One week before
Curriculum parallels other kinds of safety prevention concepts	Teach children how to avoid potentially physically or sexually abusive situations; to increase children's confidence; to deal with other dangers in order to stay as safe as possible	Not specified	To leave the children with the ability to think a situation through, make a decision that allows them to take good care of themselves
Doesn't discuss one in three or one in six statistics because staff feel they are overrated and alarming for parents. Instead focus on perpetrator	Discussion of statistics, definitions, and common misconceptions	Discussion of myths, facts, and definitions	One in three girls one in six boys. Two million children per year are physically abused (in U.S. five thousand children per week are sexually abused, about one every two minutes)
Not specified	Right to take care of their bodies	Right not to be touched in ways they feel are uncomfortable; the right to say no and the right to get help	Right to be safe
Say no, be assertive	Say no, get away, tell someone child trusts	Say no, run away, tell someone	"Stop it, get away, and tell, tell"
Call resources	How to talk with children. Parent attitudes toward disclosure. Crisis intervention. Local resources.	Call resources	Don't talk to offender. Call CPS Call resource

Table 2–3 continued

Parent Meetings	CAPP*	CSHP*	TSP*
Indicators of Abuse	—	XX	—
Why Parents Abuse/ Patterns of Abuse	—	—	—
Appropriate Discipline/ Parenting Skills	—	—	—
Information Regarding Child Abuse Reporting Laws	—	XX	XX
Sexual Abuse	XX	XX	XX
Physical Abuse	—	—	XX

*CAPP = Child Assault Prevention Project; CSHP = Children's Self-Help Project; TSP = Touch Safety Program; TAT = Talking About Touching; YSAP = Youth Safety Awareness Project; CAPIE = Child Abuse Prevention, Intervention, and Education; SAFE = Stop Abuse through Family Education

Parent Curricula

All of the parent curricula are concerned with protecting children from harm. The practical methods on how to accomplish this goal differ somewhat, as shown in table 2–3. While the programs cover much of the same content, several differences stand out in their emphases. Some programs use the parent meeting as an opportunity to teach parents how to protect their children from abuse. These programs stress the weight of parents' personal obligation to their children. In contrast, other programs expect children to protect themselves, placing emphasis on the child's responsibility for her or his own safety. Still other programs recognize parents' potential to abuse their children and use the meeting as a forum to discuss parenting skills, methods of stress reduction, and appropriate disciplining techniques. Common objectives of the programs are to teach parents about the indicators of abuse, to recognize behavioral signs of an abused child, and to report appropriately children's disclosures of abuse. In general, the parent meetings seek to increase parents' knowledge of abuse and to reduce common misperceptions about the problem. All programs place a particular emphasis on information about sexual abuse.

TAT*	YSAP*	CAPIE*	SAFE*
—	XX	XX	—
—	—	—	XX
—	XX (given time)	XX	XX
XX	XX	XX — and legal protection for children	XX
XX	XX	XX	XX
—	—	—	—

XX = Subject covered, but lacking specifics.
— = not covered.

Notes

1. It is important to note that these curricula are continually undergoing revision, both spontaneously by presenters as the need or opportunity arises and in a more formal manner by curriculum authors. Therefore, it is possible that current curricula differ from those quoted here.

2. Kathy Beland, *Talking About Touching II* (Seattle: Committee for Children, 1986), 32.

3. Children's Self-Help Project, *Preschool Curriculum* (San Francisco: Children's Self-Help Project, 1985), IVa-7.

4. Sherri Patterson, *Preschool Curriculum* (Touch Safety Program, Marin County, Calif., 1986), 5. Available from Touch Safety Program, Family Service Agency, 1005 A St., San Rafael, CA 94901.

5. Beland, *Talking About Touching,* 34.

6. Children's Self-Help Project, *Preschool Curriculum,* IVa-7.

7. Beland, *Talking About Touching,* 57.

8. Project SAFE, *Preschool* (Project SAFE, Cajon Valley Union School District, May, 1986), 3. Available from Joanne Rhudy, Cajon Valley Union School District, 189 Roanoke Road, Box 1007, El Cajon, CA 92022-1007.

9. Ibid., p. 2.

10. Patterson, *Preschool Curriculum,* 21.

11. Children's Self-Help Project, *Preschool Curriculum*, IVa-5.
12. Personal communication with YSAP staff, Spring, 1987.
13. *Child Assault Prevention Training Center of Northern California Preschool Project Training Manual* (Berkeley, Calif.: CAP Training Center, 1983), 4 (hereafter referred to as CAP Training Center).
14. Patterson, *Preschool Curriculum*, 2.
15. Children's Self-Help Project, *Preschool Curriculum*, IVa-6.
16. Beland, *Talking About Touching*, 44.
17. Children's Self-Help Project, *Preschool Curriculum*, IVa-19.
18. CAP Training Center, 19.
19. Children's Self-Help Project, *Preschool Curriculum*, IVa-19.
20. Patterson, *Preschool Curriculum*, 18, 20.
21. Beland, *Talking About Touching*, 37.
22. Children's Self-Help Project, *Preschool Curriculum*, IVa-22.
23. Beland, *Talking About Touching*, 26.
24. Patterson, *Preschool Curriculum*, 25.
25. CAP Training Center, 9.
26. Patterson, *Preschool Curriculum*, 25.
27. Ibid., 28.
28. Children's Self-Help Project, *Preschool Curriculum*, IVa-7.
29. Patterson, *Preschool Curriculum*, 24–25.
30. Beland, *Talking About Touching*, 36.
31. Personal conversation with CAPIE project staff, Spring, 1987.
32. Personal conversation with YSAP project staff, Spring 1987.
33. CAP Training Center, 18.
34. Children's Self-Help Project, *Preschool Curriculum*, IVa-5.
35. Project SAFE, *Preschool,* 3.
36. Beland, *Talking About Touching*, 19.
37. CAP Training Center, 12.
38. Patterson, *Preschool Curriculum*, 26.
39. Beland, *Talking About Touching,*36.
40. CAP Training Center, 15.
41. Children's Self-Help Project, *Preschool Curriculum*, IVa-20.
42. Patterson, *Preschool Curriculum*, 31.
43. Personal conversation with CAPIE program staff, Spring, 1987.
44. Project SAFE, *Preschool,* 3.
45. Patterson, *Preschool Curriculum*, 28.
46. Children's Self-Help Project, *Preschool Curriculum*, IVa-18.
47. CAP Training Center, 12.
48. Ibid.

3
Prevention Programs: What Do Children Learn?

T he results reported in this chapter are based on data gathered from individual interviews with 118 preschool children (93 pretest and posttest and 25 posttest only) who participated in seven child abuse prevention programs. The chapter opens with a description of the research design both as it was first envisioned and then as it evolved in order to accommodate the practical considerations and limits of doing research in action settings. The discussion then turns to the study sample and the development and implementation of the children's interview instrument. The final section of the chapter analyzes the findings and their implications.

Research Design

The intent of the research was to employ a multiple group comparison design in which the performance of children receiving different curricula would be compared in order to assess which approaches were most effective for use with preschool children. As we progressed toward selecting programs for participation—both by carefully analyzing the content of their curricula and by talking with project personnel—it became clear that, while each project does indeed have some individual characteristics, on the balance their similarities outweigh their differences. This is due in large part to the fact that the legislation sponsoring the programs defines certain areas that must be covered. Also, since some basic concepts are almost universal to the field, the potential for variation is further reduced.

Another factor that limited the comparative approach came into focus as we examined the different preschools that agreed to be study participants. Each of the preschool sites tended to serve families belonging to one or another socioeconomic or sociocultural group (for details see table 2–1). Diversity among preschool populations further mitigated against cross-site comparison of curricula.

As a final consideration, it became evident that little empirical work exists documenting the ability of preschool children to comprehend the basic concepts presented by child abuse prevention programs. These baseline data are essential to program evaluation.

With these factors in mind, we altered the design of this study to reflect the similarity of program content, the diverse population served by the various primary prevention programs, and the empirical needs of the field. The children from each site will be viewed as a composite sample, combining seven somewhat homogeneous groups into one larger heterogeneous group, that more accurately represents the population of preschoolers who receive child abuse prevention programs.

Once participating programs were selected, they were asked to locate a preschool site within their service area that would allow research to be conducted. After identifying these sites, a member of the research team met with each school's director to explain the purpose of the project, to familiarize the director with the research design and child interview instruments, and to obtain information regarding the school's schedule, theoretical foundation, and organizational structure. At five of the seven schools researchers also met with teachers and aides to explain the nature of the project and to acquaint them with the study instruments.

Parental permission for child participation was sought directly at five of the seven sites. At four of them research staff spent two to three days in the school during the time children were picked up by their parents demonstrating the children's instruments and explaining the study to parents. At this point parents were given an informational letter and informed consent form to take home, read, and return later if they agreed to participate. Children at the fifth site were bused to and from school, thus precluding the approach described above. Here, a staff member attended a regular parent meeting to address the group and to speak with individual parents, offering the same information covered at other schools. At the final two schools, letters were sent home to parents with their children.

Instrument Development

One of the greatest challenges we faced was the development of *The Child Abuse Researchers' Evaluation Series* (CARE Series),[1] the linchpin of the children's assessment. The first step in developing the children's interview protocol was to review the relevant literature and to consult with child development and child evaluation specialists regarding the availability of assessment tools appropriate to our purpose. We sought measures to assess the preschoolers' ability to grasp concepts dealing with abuse prevention. We also looked for measures of anxiety since there was concern that the presentation of abuse prevention programs to young children might raise their level of anxiety.[2] A review of research literature yielded no standardized instruments dealing with either of these areas for the preschool child,[3] making it necessary to design our own instruments.

We were well aware of the enormity of the problem being addressed and wanted to develop tools that appealed to the children, remained sensitive to their potential reactions to the subject matter, and were nonthreatening while thoroughly covering prevention material. We took note of Piaget's words: "In psychology one must speak to children in their own language, otherwise the experiment resolves itself into a trial of intelligence or of verbal understanding."[4] We sought an approach that would integrate their language with ours so that we could obtain the relevant information while putting our very young subjects at ease. The instruments needed to be developmentally appropriate.[5] Also, since many of the programs use puppets, dolls, posters, and other visual aids, we wanted to remain within the spirit set by the children's workshops. Finally, it was important that the tools appealed to the child-care providers and preschool teachers whose children we sought as participants. We were dealing with a delicate subject and anticipated that there would be concerns regarding the content and structure of the children's interviews.

With these concerns in mind, we reviewed the written curricula available for each of the programs to determine their dominant concepts. At the same time, we examined the methods of presentation used by the seven programs (that is, puppets, posters, and dolls) to avoid having the assessment approach favor any one program. It was important to test the children's ability to generalize the information conveyed by the programs to situations beyond the common stereotypes (such as accepting candy from strangers). We wanted instruments that would tap a young child's ability to generalize and to apply prevention concepts.

The next step was to decide on the specific materials we would use to test the preschool children. Using a small group of children who were within the target age range, the research team first tried storytelling with a variety of puppets and pictures, requesting story completion from the children. A second approach involved the design of pretend scenarios to be played out with the use of miniature toys. These sessions were videotaped and reviewed by the research team and other members of the Family Welfare Research Group. It was evident that the children found the puppets inviting but were more interested in playing with them than in responding to open-ended stories in a manner useful to us. Miniature toys and bright pictures seemed to hold the most promise as tools that would focus the children's attention and provide a variety of age appropriate approaches. These materials formed the basis for the final assessment tools.

With this foundation knowledge we went on to develop the CARE Series, an integrated group of assessment instruments designed to evaluate the effectiveness and appropriateness of child sexual abuse prevention programs for preschool children ages three and one-half to five years. Administration of the series would be on an individual basis and take approximately twenty minutes. After assessing the amount of time the prevention programs allocate to the major concepts presented, we decided to allot approximately one-fourth of the interview time to the anxiety scale, one-half to an integration of the Touch Continuum (feelings, secrets, and support systems), and the final fourth to strangers.

Since there is compelling evidence that children under the age of six respond with greatest spontaneity and ease to animal stimuli in contrast to human stimuli,[6] the CARE Series has an interwoven rabbit theme with colorful rabbit pictures and wooden figures. It involves an integration of several approaches to child assessment, which consist of pictures and a semistructured interview schedule to which children are asked to respond. The parameters of response are more circumscribed than those of instruments such as the Children's Apperception Test.[7] The questions posed to the child have qualities similar to those used in sentence and story completion tests.[8] Like the Peabody Picture Vocabulary Test, aspects of the instruments can be responded to nonverbally.[9]

Through the use of a neutral animal, the instrument is suitable for use with children from all cultural backgrounds. Situations presented are universal to childhood and know no socioeconomic boundaries. While the consistent use of rabbits as visual and story stimuli maintains a sense of continuity throughout the series, each section is marked by a change in activity. The varied activities keep the child on task and recognize the fact that preschool children respond well to situations in which their inclination toward physical, nonverbal expression is taken into consideration.

Once the tools were developed and an interview schedule was prepared, we piloted the CARE Series at two preschool settings, interviewing a total of forty-six preschoolers. Interviews were conducted on an individual basis, with one staff member interviewing and one staff member observing the children's responses and keeping a log of any recommendations for changes or adaptations.

During this process we refined the script so that we could best engage the child. Two anxiety scales and two picture books with slightly different scripts and pictures were used, and the children were divided into two groups balanced as closely as possible for age and sex. In this way we were able to look at alternative ways of presenting the instrument and to work toward establishing the most appropriate and efficient approach to each section of the series. We interviewed and consulted with teachers and parents to obtain collaborative information regarding the children in the pilot group in order to help determine whether the children's responses reflected their usual behavior.

We revised the initial questions and subsequent probes until we felt that the instrument addressed the concepts adequately, thereby yielding relevant responses. Child after child indicated that he or she equated the bunny pictures with his or her own experiences, making statements such as "He's happy 'cause he's tickling him. When my daddy tickles me, I laugh." or "He's sad. I don't like my sister hitting me." We found that the pictures yielded quite a range of responses. Some children offered full and elaborate explanations such as the little bunny is happy " 'cause he's hugging his mother and feels a happy feeling inside" or the little bunny is sad "because he doesn't want to take a bath because he thinks he's already clean," while others indicated only an affective state and did not offer an explanation.

The terminology was refined to convey concepts without leading the children. For example, we found it most fruitful to introduce the large rabbit in the section known as the "Stranger Story" as a "big rabbit the little bunny doesn't know" rather than as a stranger. The term *stranger* seemed to be so familiar to the children that we were not sure whether they were reacting to the term or to the situation presented. In piloting, we found that the scenario did stimulate stranger awareness responses from some of the children, indicating both knowledge and avoidance skills. For example, one child spoke of the possibility of kidnappers, another spoke of the need to check with a parent before accepting anything from a stranger, and a third demonstrated running away, stating, "No way. I'm running." A little girl fell into the spirit of the rabbits and firmly refused carrots: "No, because I have lots of carrots at home. I don't want to spoil my appetite for lettuce and cabbage."

The final step in the instrument development was the establishment of a coding system that allowed us to classify and quantify the children's responses based on the type of affect they assigned to each situation and the manner in which they explained their choices. The explanation of choices was coded in order to assess how well the children were able to connect feeling states with interpersonal interactions and touches and the extent to which this changed at posttest.

During the piloting phase of the project, the coding schemes were refined to achieve response categories that were mutually exclusive and exhaustive. During the course of the study, all the children's interviews were audiotaped and postcoded by the interviewer who conducted the interview. The coding form enabled interviewers to record all comments made by the child and the interviewer, as well as to code responses. A master list of responses and appropriate coding was kept so that identical responses were coded correctly. To maintain interrater reliability, one interviewer read each coded interview form. If she had any question about how a particular response was coded, she set aside the interview form prior to data entry. The interviewers met periodically as a group and went over the interview forms in question, arriving at a consensus for each item.

The CARE Series

The first instrument in the series, the "Anxiety Scale," was designed to assess the child's general level of anxiety. It was developed for the CARE Series in response to concerns voiced in the professional community that prevention programs for young children might heighten their anxiety. The instrument consists of a large cardboard rabbit with movable arms that the child positions to indicate the bunny's level of anxiety when faced with ten hypothetical situations. The situations range from nonthreatening (if its mother read it a story) to ambiguous (if another bunny whispered something in its ear) to threatening (if it heard grown-ups yelling very loud). By physically moving the arms of the Anxiety Bunny or by verbally responding, children indicated whether the bunny would be "very scared and worried" with its hands over its eyes and ears (score = 3), a "little bit scared and worried" with its hands extended out to its sides (score = 2), or "not scared or worried at all" with its hands on its lap (score = 1). A total score for all ten situations could range from 10 (indicating responses of "not scared" to all ten situations) to 30 (indicating responses of "very scared" to every situation).

The second instrument, the "Bunny Book," consists of colorful pictures depicting rabbits in commonly experienced human situations and rabbits expressing familiar emotions. The book covers four concepts dominant in most programs: the Touch Continuum, secrets, support systems, and self-assertion. The Touch Continuum is viewed from two perspectives, with the children first asked to identify the initial emotional response to a specific form of interpersonal physical contact (hugging, tickling, bathing, and hitting) and then to describe how the response might change. Second, the children are shown a picture of the little bunny displaying a definite emotional response (sad, mixed-up, or happy) and asked to name the touch that caused the response, with subsequent inquiry into sources of help and solace.

The final instrument in the series consists of a "Stranger Story" acted out by a set of wooden rabbits. This taps into the child's level of stranger wariness and self-assertion. Taking into consideration a preschooler's limited attention span and tendency to become restless after a period of concentration, this section encourages active participation in maneuvering figures and responding to progressively risky lures. However, the quieter child can also complete the series of questions with equal ease. The child is asked to manipulate a little bunny who is approached first by a big rabbit it doesn't know. The big rabbit asks the little bunny if it wants to pet the big rabbit's duck before they continue their walk. The little bunny is then approached by another big rabbit it doesn't know whose lures with a "nice carrot" escalate toward the potentially dangerous.

The principal variables of interest in the "Bunny Book" and the "Stranger Story" are the child's initial and subsequent abilities to (1) distinguish among the different types of touches (such as good, bad, or confusing), (2) recognize that a specific touch may generate a spectrum of responses depending on differing circumstances, (3) understand the concepts of receiving and revealing secrets, (4) be aware of potential dangers possibly inherent in interactions with strangers, and (5) demonstrate age appropriate coping strategies and self-assertion skills.

Interview Process

Before the prevention programs were presented to children, the research staff spent a day or two at each school site as participant observers. This allowed the researchers to interact with the school staff and become a familiar figure to the children in preparation for their interviews. At the start of the interviews, we arranged to have a teacher tell each child, when it was his or her turn, that it was all right to go with the interviewer. Interviews were held in the office, in a staff room, or in other areas where they could be conducted without diversion or interruption. Each lasted about twenty minutes. Posttest interviews were held four to six weeks after the children had received the training.

A total of 123 children were individually interviewed at pretest. Of these children, 112 completed the interview (see table 3–1). Interviews were terminated early if the child had difficulty attending to the task, if the child requested to return to the classroom, or if the child became concerned or upset.

Of those children who completed the pretest, ninety-three also completed the posttest. This group of ninety-three children comprises the experimental sample reported on in this study. The attrition from pretest to posttest occurred for several reasons: (1) several children moved or withdrew from school, (2) a few children were absent at the time of the presentation or at posttest, (3) two children were reported by research staff for abuse, and (4) seven children were dropped when one of the two classroom teachers at a school site withdrew from the program.

An additional twenty-five children made up the posttest-only control group. The seven projects were represented fairly evenly in the pre/post experimental group, while the post-only control group was distributed unevenly among the projects.

Table 3–1
Interviews Started and Completed

Project	Pretest		Posttest		Post-only	
	C*	S*	C	S	C	S
CAPP†	16	19	14	15	4	4
CHSP†	16	19	15	16	4	4
TSP†	17	17	15	16	3	3
TAT†	15	16	8	8	5	5
CAPIE†	17	20	15	15	1	1
YSAP†	14	17	10	11	1	1
SAFE†	17	18	16	16	7	7
Total	112	123	93	97	25	25

*C = completed; S = started

†CAPP = Child Assault Prevention Project; CHSP = Children's Self-Help Program; TSP = Touch Safety Program; TAT = Talking About Touching; CAPIE = Child Abuse Prevention, Intervention and Education; YSAP = Youth Safety Awareness Project; SAFE = Stop Abuse through Family Education

Information on race and sex is available only for the pre/post group. There was an even distribution of boys and girls. Fifty-two percent of the children were white. The majority of the other children were black. The subsample of black children comprised 25 percent of the entire sample. Three of the sites had predominantly white children participating in the study; three sites had predominately black, Hispanic, and Asian children participating; and one site had an even distribution among whites and other groups. Since the children's socioeconomic status tend to divide along school lines and is highly correlated with ethnicity, it is difficult to separate the effects of socioeconomic status and ethnic identity on the children's or parents' outcomes. At the time of pretest, the children ranged in age from three years four months to five years six months.

What the Children Learned

The following analysis focuses on the influence of the prevention programs on the knowledge, skills, and attitudes of the ninety-three preschoolers in the experimental group. The twenty-five children in the posttest-only group served as a control for the possible learning effects of the pretest interview. No significant differences were expected between the posttest scores for the pre/post group and the post-only group.

Anxiety Scores

Using the "Anxiety Scale," we had one specific area of interest: whether a young child's experience participating in a child abuse prevention program had an effect on his or her level of anxiety. The mean anxiety score increased slightly from 20.25 on pretest to 20.90 on posttest. This difference is not statistically significant ($t = 1.47, p = .15$). There was no significant difference between the experimental group and the post-only group ($t = 1.10, p = .28$). In addition, there were no significant differences between the mean scores by project.

This finding indicates that to the extent that this instrument reliably measures anxiety, the children did not experience an increase in general anxiety after exposure to child abuse prevention programs. One proviso should be added here. While it may indeed be the case that the children's anxiety level remained unchanged, it is possible that the limited degrees of discrimination afforded by this instrument in its current form may not be sensitive enough to pick up any subtle changes that may have occurred due to participation in a prevention program.

Bunny Book

The Touching Series. The first section of the "Bunny Book" contains four pictures of a big rabbit and a little rabbit engaged in interpersonal interactions that involve touching:

The two bunnies hugging

The big bunny tickling the little bunny

The big bunny bathing the little bunny

The big bunny hitting the little bunny

The little bunny has an expressionless felt face held to the page by a piece of Velcro. At the bottom of each page are three removable felt faces (see figure 3–1) also held in place by Velcro: a smiling face (happy), a face with the mouth going up and down in a sideways S (confused or mixed-up), and a frowning face (sad, angry, scared, or worried). This third expression symbolically encompasses all affective states that would fall under the classification of negative affect and represents emotional states experienced as troublesome or disturbing.

The four pictures were designed to examine the extent to which participation in a child abuse prevention project affects the subject's perceptions of everyday ambiguous and unambiguous situations. There was some concern that, as an unanticipated consequence of prevention projects, young children might come to perceive familiar, unambiguous interpersonal encounters (such as hugging) as negative or that ambiguous situations (such as tickling) that had previously been seen as positive might come to be seen as generating a sense of sadness or fear.[10] We also were interested in determining how well the children understood the concept of the Touch Continuum. The questions addressed by this section of the CARE Series were:

Did the children's affective perception of the four situations change from pretest to posttest? If change occurred, in which direction did it go? Was the change statistically significant?

Figure 3–1. Affective States

How well could the children differentiate among a good touch, a confusing touch, and a bad touch? Did their ability to do this improve from pretest to posttest?

Did the children's ability to give a logical explanation for attributing a specific affective state to a familiar, albeit ambiguous, situation improve after exposure to a child abuse prevention program?

These questions were operationalized by asking the child to select the felt face that represented the feelings the little bunny was experiencing regarding the four interactions (being hugged, tickled, bathed, and hit) and to put the face on the little bunny. The four different touches were selected with an eye toward offering a spectrum of interpersonal experiences. It was anticipated that the hugging picture would generate predominantly positive (happy) initial responses, that tickling and bathing would generate more varied responses, and that initial responses to hitting would be sad or angry. In the pretest, most of the children did indeed see the little bunny as happy in the hugging picture and sad in the hitting picture, but the tickling and bathing pictures also were seen as predominantly happy. At posttest, these responses changed, moving toward a gloomier view in three of the four situations. Only in the hugging picture did a higher proportion of children indicate that the little bunny felt happy at posttest (see tables 3–2a through 3–2d).

There was little evidence of change in the children's use of the mixed-up affect from pretest to posttest. Chi-square values were significant for the hugging picture ($p = .001$) and the bathing picture ($p = .006$), but interpretation of this statistical measure should be tempered by the fact that in both of these tables expected frequencies in four of the nine cells were less than 5. Convention recommends that when a high percentage of cells have expected frequencies this small, one can no longer assume the accuracy of chi-square statistics.

Table 3–2a
Change in Affect Attributed to Hugging

| | Posttest | | | |
Pretest	Happy	Mixed-up	Sad	Pretest Totals
Happy	53	3	4	60 (65.9%)
Mixed-up	5	1	4	10 (11.0%)
Sad	11	5	5	21 (23.1%)
Posttest Totals	69 (75.8%)	9 (9.9%)	13 (14.3%)	91 (100.0%)

Table 3–2b
Change in Affect Attributed to Tickling

| | Posttest | | | |
Pretest	Happy	Mixed-up	Sad	Pretest Totals
Happy	40	5	19	64 (70.3%)
Mixed-up	3	3	6	12 (13.2%)
Sad	7	2	6	15 (16.5%)
Posttest Totals	50 (54.9%)	10 (11.0%)	31 (34.1%)	91 (100.0%)

Table 3–2c
Change in Affect Attributed to Bathing

| | Posttest | | | |
Pretest	Happy	Mixed-up	Sad	Pretest Totals
Happy	45	6	12	63 (68.5%)
Mixed-up	3	4	5	12 (13.0%)
Sad	6	5	6	17 (18.5%)
Posttest Totals	54 (58.7%)	15 (16.3%)	23 (25.0%)	92 (100.0%)

Table 3–2d
Change in Affect Attributed to Hitting

| | Posttest | | | |
Pretest	Happy	Mixed-up	Sad	Pretest Totals
Happy	3	0	17	20 (22.2%)
Mixed-up	2	0	7	9 (10.0%)
Sad	2	5	54	61 (67.8%)
Posttest Totals	7 (7.8%)	5 (5.6%)	78 (86.7%)	90 (100.0%)

To determine the extent to which the pretest might have influenced the change in the children's responses, the distribution of scores for the experimental group at posttest and the posttest-only control group were examined. If the pretest did not influence the change, one would expect the difference in the posttest response rates to be nonsignificant, which was the case for all four pictures. These findings suggest a tendency for children to be more likely to interpret frequently encountered interactions as evoking a negative affect after participation in prevention training.

To ascertain the extent to which young children can grasp the logical connection between experiencing a touch and experiencing an emotional feeling related either to the touch or the individual doing the touching, we probed further and asked the child why the little bunny might have felt happy, mixed-up, or sad about the touch. The children's descriptive responses were coded into three categories.

Correspondence. The child's explanation of the reason the little bunny feels happy, mixed-up, or sad corresponds with the affect selected and with the touch depicted.

Hugging Picture
Happy response—" 'Cause his daddy's hugging him." "He likes to be happy and wants to be hugged."

Mixed-up response—"Because he doesn't like what the person is doing."

Sad response—"He doesn't like to hug because people always hug him too tight."

Tickling Picture
Happy response—" 'Cause he tickle. When someone tickle me, I laugh." "He's getting ticklish 'cause his dad is playing with him."

Mixed-up response—"It makes them fall down but he's not crying or nothing."

Sad response—" 'Cause he doesn't want anybody to tickle him."

Bathing Picture
Happy response—"He's in the bath and his mom's washing him with his little duck." " 'Cause the big bunny's bathing him."

Mixed-up response—"He's in the bathtub and somebody going to take him out."

Sad response—"He didn't want to take a bath because the bath is too hot." " 'Cause the daddy's not bathing her and she has to wash her hair by herself."

Hitting Picture
Mixed-up response—"He doesn't want to get hit." "Because he can't remember if she's hitting him or tickling him."

Sad response—"Mad. He has a mad face and a sad face 'cause it hurts." " 'Cause he's punching. They wouldn't let him play basketball."

Noncorrespondence. The child's explanation of the reason the little bunny feels happy, mixed-up, or sad does not correspond with the affect selected or the touch depicted but is the opposite of it.

Hugging Picture
Mixed-up response—"He loves his mother."

Sad response—"He's hugging and kissing."

Hitting Picture
Happy response—"His mama's hitting him."

Unrelated. The response is unrelated to the picture, although it may fit the affect selected.

Hugging Picture
Happy response—"He saw his friends."

Tickling Picture
Happy response—"He made something." "He's playing with the blocks."

Sad response—"He wants to be." "He had a dream."

Bathing Picture
Sad response—" 'Cause I gave that face to him."

Hitting Picture
Happy response—" 'Cause there's a ball there."

Sad response—"He wanted to play basketball." "The bird is saying stop."

Table 3–3 shows the children's descriptive verbal responses as categorized above. The noncorrespondence and unrelated responses have been collapsed into the single "other response" category.

The differences between the children's pretest and posttest scores for the experimental group are significant for two of the four pictures, suggesting that the programs only moderately helped children to connect affect better with a specific situation involving touching. In addition, the distribution of scores by category for the experimental posttest and the posttest-only control group show a significant difference on two of the four pictures (hugging and tickling). This raises a question about the extent to which the experimental group's increased pattern of logical correspondence at posttest may be attributed to

Table 3–3
Logical Correspondence between Touching and Affect

Picture	Pretest (n = 93)	Posttest (n = 93)	Post-only (n = 25)
Hug			
Correspondence	61.3%	78.5%	48.0%
Other response	38.7%	21.5%	52.0%
Chi-square*			
Pre/post: 6.54, p = .0105			
Post/post-only: 9.10, p = .0026			
Tickle			
Correspondence	71.0%	82.8%	56.0%
Other response	29.0%	17.2%	44.0%
Chi-square*			
Pre/post: 3.66, p = .0557			
Post/post-only: 8.02, p = .0046			
Bath			
Correspondence	63.4%	68.8%	64.0%
Other response	36.6%	31.2%	36.0%
Chi square*			
Pre/post: .60, p = .4385			
Post/post-only: .21, p = .6472			
Hit			
Correspondence	60.2%	71.0%	56.0%
Other response	39.8%	29.0%	44.0%
Chi square*			
Pre/post: 2.38, p = .1227			
Post/post-only: 2.02, p = .1550			

*Chi-square values for pretest/posttest differences and for posttest/posttest-only control group differences are based on the marginal totals reported above, which reflect directional change by category of responses.

the prevention programs. It is possible, for example, that the experimental group experienced a learning effect from the pretest, thus enabling them to achieve higher scores on correspondence the second time they were tested. In the same vein, by exposing the children to stimuli closely related to child abuse prevention program concepts, the pretest may have heightened their awareness of these areas, making them more receptive to the program's messages and subsequently better able to respond to the CARE Series at the posttest.

Looking more closely at the children's ability to link touch and emotion, their responses were combined across the four pictures to yield a composite score. Each corresponding response was awarded one point. On pretest 34.4 percent of the children in the experimental group gave logical responses to all four pictures, while on the posttest, this increased to 50.5 percent. Overall, there was a statistically significant increase (t = 3.29, p = .011) in the mean score from a pretest average of 2.56 to a posttest of 3.01. This difference suggests that the training program had some positive influence on children's ability to recognize logical connections between touching and feelings, but this interpretation of the findings must be tempered by the fact that, as shown in table 3–4, the post-only control group mean is significantly lower than the experimental group's posttest mean ($t = 2.31, p = .027$). Again, the control group findings suggest that some of the increase in the experimental group scores may be related to a learning effect from the pretest.

In general, the findings show that many of the children in this sample were capable of identifying an emotion that they associated with a particular touch and of creating a story to explain their choice. It is important to bear in mind, however, that discounting the learning effect, even at posttest half of the children in the experimental group were not able to provide a logical explanation for a response that they chose on all pictures. It is difficult to ascertain the extent to which this is due to developmental limitations in the children's language skills or their inability to understand the concepts under investigation here. If the latter is the case, this finding has serious implications in regard to child abuse prevention training, for the majority of the programs seek to convey a firm understanding of the Touch Continuum and the ability to identify a spectrum of touches. It is with this knowledge and awareness that the child is enabled to respond to his or her inner feelings and reactions and heed the further teachings of the program: Say no. Run. Tell.

Drawing together both the differences in affect attributed to the little bunny and the change in logical correspondence, the findings were examined from another perspective. On differences in affect, the trend was for children to view all but the hugging picture as sadder at posttest than at pretest. The children's ability to explain the emotional response they attributed to various situations seemed to increase from pretest to posttest. The following questions now arise: Were the children more capable of formulating corresponding responses for one of the affective levels than the others? Did their areas of correspondence remain consistent from pretest to posttest?

To answer these questions, we calculated the pretest and posttest rates of corresponding responses per affect on each picture. As table 3–5 shows,

Table 3–4
Composite Scores on Logical Correspondence between Touching and Affect

Score	Pretest (n = 93)	Posttest (n = 93)	Post-only (n = 25)
0	14.0%	7.5%	20.0%
1	8.6%	5.4%	16.0%
2	19.4%	16.1%	12.0%
3	23.6%	20.4%	24.0%
4	34.4%	50.5%	28.0%
Mean	2.56	3.01	2.24

Table 3–5
Percentage of Correspondence
for Each Affect State Pretest and Posttest

Picture	Pretest	Posttest
Hugging		
Happy	70.0%	70.0%
	(n = 60)*	(n = 70)
Mixed-up	63.64%	22.22%
	(n = 11)	(n = 9)
Sad	38.10%	69.23%
	(n = 21)	(n = 13)
Tickling		
Happy	72.30%	86.6%
	(n = 65)	(n = 50)
Mixed-up	83.33%	72.72%
	(n = 12)	(n = 11)
Sad	60.0%	83.87%
	(n = 15)	(n = 31)
Bathing		
Happy	70.31%	70.37%
	(n = 64)	(n = 54)
Mixed-up	33.33%	46.67%
	(n = 12)	(n = 7)
Sad	58.82%	82.60%
	(n = 17)	(n = 23)
Hitting		
Happy	0.00%	0.00%
	(n = 2)	(n = 1)
Mixed-up	55.55%	40.00%
	(n = 9)	(n = 5)
Sad	81.97%	80.00%
	(n = 61)	(n = 80)

*n = number of responses attempted per affect

the happy response has a steady and moderately high level of correspondence at all points except on the tickling picture, which rose considerably at posttest. The mixed-up response was seldom given, had a more erratic pattern of correspondence, ranging from 22.2 percent to 83.3 percent, and evidenced a definite decrease in correspondence from pretest to posttest on three of the pictures. The sad affect moved in the direction of a marked increase in correspondence on the first three pictures. On the hitting picture, the movement (albeit very slight) was toward decreased correspondence. It is notable that the pretest responses on this picture were already showing a high degree of correspondence.

In sum, after participation in prevention training, the children viewed the situations as sad more frequently than at pretest and were more able to give logical reasons for this perception. Not only were they seeing more negative affect in the pictures, they were describing it with a higher degree of precision.

In the lessons on good and bad touches, prevention programs address the idea that one's feelings about physical contact might change under different circumstances. To determine how well the children understood that a touch could change in degrees (for example, hugging harder or softer) or elicit different feelings, they were asked to imagine what might cause the little bunny's feelings to change from one state to another: "The big bunny is (hugging, tickling, bathing, hitting) the little bunny. The little bunny is (happy, mixed-up, sad). What could happen to make the little bunny feel (opposite emotion)? What could happen to make the little bunny feel (remaining emotion)?" The children's responses fell into three categories: change of action, change of feeling, and change of circumstance.

Hugging Picture
Happy—"He likes hugging."

Change to sad—"He doesn't like it anymore." (change of feeling)

Change to mixed-up—"I don't know."

Tickling Picture
Happy—"He likes tickles."

Change to sad—"His mama tickled him and he was sad. His mama tickled him all day."

Change to mixed-up—"His mama said stand up and I'll tickle you." (change of action)

Bathing Picture
Happy—"He likes taking a bath."

Change to sad—"Someone punched him." (change of action)

Change to mixed-up—"I don't know."

Happy—"He likes being in the warm water."

Change to sad—"If he wasn't in the warm water and he was in the cold water." (change of circumstance)

Change to mixed-up—"If the water was warm and cold. Kind of warmish-coldish." (change of circumstance)

Hitting Picture
Sad—"He doesn't like it when he's hit."

Change to happy—"If he wasn't being hit." (change of action)

Change to mixed-up—"I don't know."

The concept of alternate feelings under different circumstances was difficult for the preschoolers to grasp. Sixty percent of the sample were not asked the two follow-up questions on all pictures. Interviewers did not pursue this line of questioning if (1) the child had been unable to respond to that particular feeling in previous pictures (usually the confused feeling), (2) the child had undue difficulty in responding to these questions, or (3) the child lost interest in that picture and wanted to turn the page.

The children were awarded one point for each logical response identifying the little bunny's change of affect, and the scores were combined across the four pictures. Possible scores ranged from 0 to 8 representing two attempts for each of four pictures. On the pretest 44.1 percent of the children were able to provide two or more logical responses out of the eight attempts; on the posttest this percentage increased to 54.8 percent (table 3–6). While this represents a statistically significant increase in scores from a pretest mean of 1.7 to a posttest mean of 2.67 ($t = 4.03, p < .0001$), the change is negligible when the possible range of scores is taken into consideration. Also, there was a significant difference between the posttest means for the experimental group and the means for the post-only control group ($t = 3.03, p = .004$), which again points to the possibility that the children had experienced a learning effect from the pretest.

Secrets. The second section of the "Bunny Book" focuses on a picture and questions regarding secrets. The prevention programs attempt to teach children that there are different kinds of secrets, that touching that makes them uncomfortable should never be kept a secret, and that the child should tell any secret that makes him or her uncomfortable. In many ways secrets are used as what might be called an auditory touch. In prevention parlance one treats a secret in a manner similar to a touch. It is necessary to discriminate between good and bad secrets as well as to know what to do when told one.

Table 3–6
Composite Score on Ability to Identify Change of Affect

Score	Pretest (n = 93)	Posttest (n = 93)	Post-only (n = 25)
0	38.7%	30.1%	48.0%
1	17.2%	15.1%	24.0%
2	17.2%	9.7%	16.0%
3	6.5%	7.5%	4.0%
4	7.5%	8.6%	—
5	10.8%	12.9%	—
6	—	6.5%	4.0%
7	2.2%	4.3%	—
8	—	5.4%	4.0%
Mean	1.70	2.67	1.24

The secret picture shows the big bunny whispering into the little bunny's ear. The little bunny has a confused expression. The interviewer says: "The big bunny has told the little bunny something and has told the little bunny not to tell anyone. The little bunny looks all mixed-up. What do you think the big bunny told the little bunny? What do you think the little bunny should do?"

The child is initially asked what the big bunny told the little bunny. We expected the children to be able to imagine something that the big bunny might have said, in response to the brief story offered. Only eleven children (11.8 percent) were able to do this on pretest. Good secrets such as "He loves him" or "He'd give him a Popsicle" accounted for four of these statements, while the other seven were bad secrets such as "He told him not to play with someone else." On posttest twenty-one (22.6 percent) of the children were able to imagine a secret in response to the question. Five of these were good secrets and sixteen were bad secrets. More than 40 percent of the children were not able to give any answer, and many could repeat only what the interviewer had told them, stating, "He told him not to tell." One wonders whether their imaginations are not advanced enough at this age to invent what the bunny said or whether the children were so concrete that they ignored the "something" that the big bunny said and focused instead on the fact that he "told the little bunny not to tell." Thus, their answers are technically correct.

The children were then asked whether the little bunny should tell someone what the big bunny said. The pretest and posttest responses to this question were significantly different (chi-square = 6.37, p = .0116), with the proportion of children who thought the bunny should tell increasing from 45.2 percent at pretest to 55.9 percent at posttest. Of those children who reported that the little bunny should tell someone, the majority thought it should be an adult (parent, teacher, or another big bunny). Even at posttest, however, close to 50 percent of the children thought the little bunny should not tell anyone what the big bunny said. Considering the fact that all the prevention programs discuss secrets to tell and not to tell, one must question how well these children are able to understand this concept.

In presenting this scenario, we did not use the word *secret* in the initial questions in order to give the children an opportunity to offer the word spontaneously. Only ten children (10.8 percent) did this on pretest, and eleven children (11.8 percent) did so on posttest. After answering the questions about whether the little bunny should tell, children who had not mentioned the word *secret* were asked, "Did the big bunny tell the little bunny a secret?" On pretest sixty-three children (67.7 percent) agreed that the big bunny had. As shown in table 3–7, there were no significant differences between pretest and posttest responses to this question. After participation in the prevention programs almost 25 percent of the children still failed to recognize being told not to tell anyone as being a secret.

Table 3–7
Recognition of Secret

	Pretest (n = 93)	Posttest (n = 93)
Spontaneously	10.8%	11.8%
When asked	67.7%	63.4%
Did not identify	21.5%	24.7%

Chi-square: 1.1, p = .8994

Fixed Expression and Support Systems. The final section of the "Bunny Book" contains three pictures of the little bunny alone on the page. The first bunny is depicted as sad, the second as mixed-up, and the third as happy (see figure 3–1). Each picture is introduced by the interviewer: "Someone touched this little bunny. The little bunny feels sad (mixed-up/happy) about the touch. I wonder what happened. What do you think happened to this sad (mixed-up/happy) little bunny?"

Here the intention is to ascertain the childen's level of comprehension of the Touch Continuum by offering an affective reaction and asking the child to describe or name the touch—an approach opposite that taken in the first section. These touches were then categorized as bad touches ("Somebody's been messing with him." "Someone hit her in the face and wanted her to fall down and fall down on the swings." "Doesn't like being touched." "Hard touch."), confusing touches ("He was touched by a stranger." "He changed his mind." "He hitted him and then he kissed him."), and good touches ("He likes the touch." "Pet him soft." "His mom and dad touched him with a cute, cute happy touch.").

Table 3–8 compares the replies regarding the types of touch the children linked to different states of affect in the pretest and posttest. The data here reveal an increase in the ability to identify touches appropriate to the states of affect depicted in each of the three pictures. The largest gain was registered on the sad face. This parallels the findings on the earlier part of the touching

Table 3–8
Children's Comprehension of Affect
(percent able to give appropriate response for each picture*)

Picture	Pretest (n = 93)	Posttest (n = 93)	Post-only (n = 25)
Sad Face	33.4%	53.9%	36.0%
Mixed-up face	16.1%	36.6%	28.0%
Happy face	41.9%	50.5%	32.0%

*Sad face: Bad/sad touch or confused touch; Mixed-up face: Bad/sad touch, confused touch, happy/good touch; Happy face: Happy/good touch or confused touch series, which suggested that perceptions of negative affect were amplified by participation in prevention training. However, the data in table 3–8 also show that the posttest-only control group scores were much closer to those of the pretest than the posttest experimental group, which raises the possibility that some degree of the change in the experimental groups might be attributed to the learning effect. In any event more than half the time the children still were unable to offer an appropriate connection between touching and different states of affect.

This section looked into the children's ability to specify suitable sources of support by inquiring how the little bunny could get help. Children were generally able to identify someone, either an adult or a peer, as being able to help. Table 3–9 shows the breakdown of the sources of help the children identified as available to the sad little bunny and the percentage of children who specified each source. As the data indicate, changes in scores for the experimental group were significant for the sad bunny, suggesting an increase in the children's ability to delineate available and appropriate sources of support in times of stress. Changes in scores were not significant for the mixed-up picture. The question was not asked concerning the happy picture.

Stranger Story

The final instrument in the CARE Series is designed to assess the child's level of stranger wariness and self-protection skills. The "Stranger Story" uses wooden figures of bunnies to enact a brief scenario that measures the general level of caution and apparent vulnerability to abduction, as well as the ability to generalize typical prevention examples.

The child is given a small bunny to manipulate while the interviewer introduces two big rabbits the little bunny doesn't know. In the first scene, a big rabbit is walking its pet duck to the park so the duck can have a quick swim before nap time. As the big rabbit approaches, it stops and asks the little bunny

Table 3–9
Sources of Help Identified

	Pretest *(n = 76)**	*Posttest* *(n = 80)*	*Post-only* *(n = 18)*
Peer	15.8%	12.5%	11.2%
Adult	60.5%	68.8%	44.4%
Not helpful	23.7%	18.7%	44.4%

Chi-square
  Pre/post: 104.52, $p < .0001$
  Post/post-only: 72.0, $p < .0001$

*Children who, due to responses to earlier questions, were not asked this question are not included in the analysis.

if it would like to pet the duck. The interviewer asks the children what the little bunny says and does and encourages them to enact the response. The big rabbit and duck go on. A few children spontaneously had the little bunny join the big rabbit and its duck. This is not written into the script but was clearly a temptation for some children. They are then asked to return to continue the story.

The second big rabbit arrives bearing a carrot and attempts to lure the little bunny with bribes, tricks, and force (for example, "I have a nice carrot here. Would you like it?" "I have more in my car, would you like to come and see them?" "Look at all those yummy carrots. Get in and I'll take you to where they grow and you can pick some." "What if the big rabbit said, 'Your Mommy and Daddy said it is okay'?" "What if the big rabbit said, 'I'll pull you by the ears'?"). After each lure or bribe, the child is asked to enact the little bunny's response. The "What if the big bunny said . . ." questions are asked if the child states that the little bunny would say no to the previous bribe or trick. This format was chosen to avoid undermining the children's appropriate self-assertion skills and yet see whether they could be cajoled or coerced into changing their minds.

Children responded to the "Stranger Story" in various ways. Some were relatively passive, while others joined the story with gusto and action. The more passive children would say yes or no quietly, sometimes barely moving the little bunny. Others would give an enthusiastic "Yes!" when offered a carrot, lean the little bunny over to pretend to eat the carrot—often accompanied by eating sounds—and hold the big rabbit's hand on the way to the car, which they rode in with accompanying motor noise. Some were quite cautious. When offered the chance to pet the duck, one child said, "I have to ask my mother." The child then acted this out, gaining permission to pet the duck and go to the park. When offered the carrot by the second rabbit, she replied, "If my mom says so," and asked her mother. She continued, "My mom says no I can't take it." When invited to the car, she replied, "No. I can't take nothing from strangers." Another child was polite. To petting the duck, she said, "I don't know that duckie." When offered the carrot, she stated, "No thank you." The invitation to go to the car elicited a louder "No thank you." When the big rabbit threatened to pull the little bunny by the ears, the little bunny ran home. When the child was asked what the little bunny would do if the big rabbit told her that her parents said it was all right, she replied, "Okay. That's like it was a baby-sitter."

A little boy was reluctant to let the little bunny pet the duck. "Well, all right. Oh, you're not a stranger, are you? Oh, I know, you're a stranger. I'm not going to pet you." To the offer of a carrot, he replied, "Sure, I love carrots." When invited to the car, he replied, "Are you a stranger? I think, I think, I think you're my dad. All right, I'll come in the car with you." When asked what the little bunny would do if the big rabbit were a stranger, the boy wouldn't let the little bunny cooperate. It is interesting to note that this child introduced an unanticipated element to these stories: the noncustodial parent and potential abduction. Four children (a small sample, to be sure) allowed the little bunny to go with the big rabbit, letting it be known that the little bunny thought it was Daddy. These children also had shown some yearning for the missing parent in their responses to the pictures in the "Bunny Book." In the parent interviews, all of their mothers had indicated experiencing a stressful separation.

The children's responses to the "Stranger Story" are shown in table 3–10. These data indicate that the children were less likely to allow the little bunny to accept the carrot and to accompany the carrot-bearing rabbit to its car or to get into the car at posttest than they were at pretest. In addition, the children were less likely to allow the little bunny to acquiesce to the big rabbit's trickery or force at posttest than at pretest.

We avoided the term *stranger* throughout the scenario script for two reasons. First, during the pilot test it became clear that this word served as an immediate stimulus for specific responses. It gave many children a clear cue about the reaction expected to the approach of the big rabbits. Second, we were interested in finding out whether the children could identify a stranger on their own and then act in a way consistent with prevention teachings. A small proportion of the children were able to identify the big rabbit as a stranger, and a much larger proportion recognized the potential danger inherent in following the big rabbit and getting into the car. Thus, it is evident that the stranger label is not crucial to a child's recognition of possible danger. Sometimes it has no apparent effect. At least one child, for example, quizzed his interviewer intently at the approach of the first big rabbit, trying to ascertain whether it was a stranger. He was told he could choose what it was. He stated that it was a stranger. He then proceeded to pet the duck, go to the park, take the carrot, and go to the car.

A composite score of the children's responses to the "Stranger Story" was developed. Each time a child did not allow the bunny to engage itself with a

Table 3–10
Responses to Stranger Story

	Pretest (n = 93)	Posttest (n = 93)	Post-only (n = 25)
Did not pet duck	20.4%	28.0%	36.0%
Did not follow duck to park	87.1%	81.7%	88.0%
Did not take carrot	19.4%	28.0%	32.0%
Did not go to car	18.3%	38.7%	40.0%
Did not get into car	25.8%	41.9%	52.0%
Did not go if violence used (pulling ear)	23.7%	37.6%	52.0%
Did not go when tricked	14.0%	23.7%	48.0%
Identified rabbit as stranger	8.6%	12.4%	4.0%

Table 3–11
Composite Scores on Stranger Scenario

Score	Pretest (n = 93)	Posttest (n = 93)	Post-only (n = 25)
0	11.8%	14.0%	—
1	50.5%	36.6%	36.0%
2	9.7%	3.2%	12.9%
3	4.3%	6.5%	4.0%
4	3.2%	6.5%	12.0%
5	3.2%	10.8%	8.0%
6	15.1%	11.8%	8.0%
7	2.2%	6.5%	16.0%
8	—	4.3%	4.0%
Mean	2.1720	2.9247	3.520

stranger (for example, not taking a carrot from the rabbit), the child received one point. The child could receive a total of seven points for stranger avoidance, and an additional point was awarded if the child spontaneously recognized that the big rabbit whom the little bunny doesn't know was a stranger to the little bunny.

When the children's scores on each item were combined, we found a statistically significant ($t = 3.32$, $p = .001$) increase from a pretest mean of 2.17 to a posttest mean of 2.92, as reported in table 3–11. One should not draw the substantive conclusion that this indicates that the children learned a great deal from the stranger danger lessons. The total possible score is 8; while the experimental posttest group did improve, half the children still did not get more than one point on the scale. No significant difference was found between the posttest group and the post-only group.

While the children's level of stranger wariness increased from pretest to posttest, overall it remained low. The majority of them still indicated at posttest that it would be all right for the little bunny to accept a trip in a car with a big rabbit it doesn't know, implying that these children have low stranger avoidance skills. In bringing the children's interview to a close, we added a brief message at the end of the posttest "Stranger Story." If the child had allowed the little bunny to acquiesce to the big rabbit in any way, Mother Rabbit was introduced. She enlisted the child's help in reviewing the never talk to or go with strangers rule for the little bunny. In this way we hoped to avoid leaving the children with the impression that they had played a game with a friendly individual at school who condoned ignoring stranger danger rules.

What Do These Findings Mean?

Looking at the Touch Continuum and affective reactions, some of the children appear to have a rudimentary grasp of the concept that there is a connection between the physical act of being touched and the emotion it generates. This is a pivotal concept in child abuse prevention, for the programs work from the assumption that the children have this foundation knowledge and are prepared to build on it and learn the more abstract concept that the touch may have different connotations than those the child initially perceives. One should be cautious in interpreting this finding, however. Even at posttest half the children could not provide an explanation for the affect they selected on all the pictures. A question arises here. If the children cannot explain their own responses, is it possibly too much to expect that they can understand the subtle nuances and emotions described and elicited either during the prevention program or in a case of actual abuse? Further, the children evidenced difficulty in distinguishing how touches can change or how feelings regarding the touches can change. Here again the question of development readiness arises. It may be that preschoolers are too young to grasp this more abstract concept.

The findings also bring up the question of whether the children are ready to absorb the Touch Continuum in its entirety. Their grasp of the two extremes, good and bad touches, is solid, as seen in the fact that the majority of the children were able to identify and describe these touches with accuracy. The mixed-up or confusing touch was beyond their comprehension, however. Seldom was it voluntarily attempted when the children were initially asked to state how the little bunny felt. In all instances except the tickling picture, which had been designed as an ambiguous scene, only a small proportion of the children who attempted to apply this affective response could offer a corresponding reason for stating that the little bunny felt confused. When we inquired about possible change of affect in each situation, the children could make the transition to a sad or happy state with considerably more ease than they could to a confused state. Many children could not or would not attempt this transition.

Similarly, children could describe a logical touch that might have caused the little bunny to feel confused in the second set of pictures much less often than they were able to describe touches causing sadness or happiness. They had trouble discriminating between bad touches and mixed-up ones. By far the most responses expressing confused feelings fell into the realm of negative affect or bad touches. In general, it seems that the children were not yet capable of assimilating this concept.

Concerning the children's comprehension of touches, they appeared better able to attribute a specific affective state to a situation than to describe the touch that caused the state. The task in the final section of the "Bunny Book" is to define an action based on an emotion, exactly the opposite of the task in the first section of the book. The children seemed to be better able to complete the task in the first section. The possible responses were more circumscribed for the first section, while the second section was open-ended and used some terminology that may have been vague to the children—that is, it relied on the word *touch* as the key word to which to respond. ("Someone touched the little bunny and he feels sad/mixed-up/happy. What happened to the little bunny?") It may be that the word *touch*, which frequently has connotations of a gentle contact, was not enough of a stimulus for a response that would correspond with a negative affect. A further consideration is that if the children did indeed understand the term *touch* as used in prevention, they were left with a whole range of possible actions from which to choose. Perhaps the abstract nature of the question made the task difficult for these young children. If this is the case, it seems important to look at how children understand the terminology offered by the prevention programs in order to ensure that the message is reaching them as intended.

The secret concept also is difficult for children to grasp. When we were designing the CARE Series, this area of inquiry offered the greatest challenge. Phrasing the question posed problems, as the term *tell a secret* can be applied either to the initiator of the secret or to the recipient, who then reveals it to yet another party. Throughout the questioning the children's responses indicated confusion. Many of their responses expressed the concrete thinking that marks this developmental stage. These findings open the question of how well one can expect a young child to comprehend the message conveyed in the secret concept. While they use different language, all the prevention programs explain that the basic combination of (1) being told not to tell something and (2) feeling mixed-up (uncomfortable) about it are clear signals of possible danger. This combination, as expressed in the CARE Series, did not alert almost half the children to the potential danger or stimulate them to demonstrate awareness of the necessary subsequent actions. The concept that some secrets should be told (that is, revealed) is difficult to convey. While it is important to child abuse prevention, this idea is, perhaps, beyond the capability of preschool children to comprehend or accept.

Stranger danger is one of the more unambiguous ideas presented by the child abuse prevention programs. Provided that the child is capable of recognizing a stranger, the dictum is clear: Do not talk to him or her. Do not take anything. Do not go with him or her. This lesson often is reinforced by parents and teachers. Even so, a large number of the children did not indicate that they had internalized these rules well enough to apply them.

One overall trend in the findings was the tendency for perceptions of negative affect to increase after participation in the program. This tendency is seen at several points in the study. An increase in perceptions of negative affect was registered in the first section of the "Bunny Book" where the children were asked to label the affect the little bunny was experiencing and then to give a reason for selecting that affective state. In the last section on posttest, the children were more able to give a logical response to the bunny expressing a negative affect, which brought the posttest responses to negative and positive affect about equal. In the secret picture, there was a slight gain in the children's ability to create a secret, either attributed to the big bunny or cited as a secret not to tell, which fell into the bad secret category, a category that parallels the bad touch or negative affect. As discussed earlier, it is possible that a learning effect stemming from the pretest influenced some of the posttest responses.

Interpreting the Results: A Critical Perspective

A number of critical points may be raised with regard to interpreting the study's results on the question of what children learn. These points include the following concerns:

1. The CARE Series did not measure what it is supposed to measure. Establishing validity is a common problem of social science research that seeks to measure complex phenomena with difficult subjects. In examining what the children seemed to have learned about the Touch Continuum, secrets, strangers, and support networks, how does one know whether the empirical measures obtained capture the real meaning of these ideas? Perhaps the children were responding not in terms of how they might react to the scenarios, but how they thought little bunnies might react. The CARE Series was not tested for predictive validity (such tests raise serious methodological and ethical issues, as is discussed in chapter 8). The best that can be said for this instrument is that it possesses a degree of face validity. In developing the instrument, different approaches to measurement were pretested, carefully studied, and revised. While there is still room for improving the final instrument, the children's responses convey a reasonable impression that the CARE Series affords a valid test of the central ideas taught in the prevention programs. The fact that there were two disclosures of abuse during the interviews suggests that the use of bunnies did not necessarily distort the children's reactions to the content under consideration.

2. The analysis did not control the variables to determine subgroup effects of the prevention training. Maybe the programs worked for boys but not girls, middle-class but not working-class children, four-and-one-half-year-olds but not three-and-one-half-year-olds, or some ethnic groups but not others. By analyzing the sample data without controlling for these various characteristics, it is possible that the findings overlook differential learning that took place in the programs. This is true, one would expect, particularly for the learning experiences of three-and-one-half-year-olds versus five-year-olds, although the differences, if any, probably would not be very large given the rather small gains registered overall. The basic consideration here is that there were no special curricula for three-and-one-half-year-olds, boys, girls, middle-class children, or other subgroups in the programs. The programs were assessed on their own terms.

3. The full extent of the programs' positive outcomes cannot be measured at this point in time. The view has been expressed that, at the preschool level,

the programs plant a "protective seed," the effects of which are not immediately evident.[11] This protective seed hypothesis is an article of faith. There is no evidence that any such seed has been planted or that if it has been planted it will yield the positive results claimed. On the contrary, the tendency is for learning to erode over time. This suggests that, as in our study, when children are tested immediately after exposure to the programs, the small gains in knowledge are more likely to decline over time rather than to increase.

4. The study has several limitations that qualify interpretation of its results. The sample of 118 students is relatively small, the instrument is new, and the absence of random assignment to experimental and control groups breaches the formal requirements of experimental design. While the study reveals limited gains in knowledge, which raises significant questions about preschool children's ability to grasp the content offered in prevention curricula, one must be cautious in drawing implications from these findings alone. Before reaching any firm conclusions about the value of preschool training, these findings must be assessed in light of related research on preschool prevention programs and cognitive development, as well as other implications of the prevention curricula. In addition to the findings reported here, the directions for change identified in chapter 8 are informed by a larger view of knowledge and concerns regarding what children can learn, what they do learn, and what they should learn.

Notes

1. The instrument is presented in full in the appendix.
2. Jon Conte, "Research on the Prevention of Sexual Abuse of Children" (Paper presented at the Second National Conference for Family Violence Researchers, Durham, New Hampshire, 7–10 August 1984); David Finkelhor, "Prevention: A Review of Programs and Research," in *A Sourcebook on Child Sexual Abuse,* eds. David Finkelhor and Associates (Beverly Hills: Sage Publications, 1986).
3. *J. Mitchel, ed., Ninth Mental Measurements Yearbook* (Lincoln, Neb.: Buros Institute of Mental Measurement, 1985); J. Goldman, C. Stein, and S. L'Engle, *Psychological Methods of Child Assessment* (New York: Brunner/Mazel, 1983); W. Johnson, *Preschool Test Descriptions: Test Matrix and Correlated Test Descriptions* (Springfield, Ill.: Charles C. Thomas, 1979); L. Southworth, R. Burr, and A. Cox. *Screening and Evaluating the Young Child: A Handbook of Instruments to Use from Infancy to Six Years* (Springfield, Ill.: Charles C. Thomas, 1980).
4. Jean Piaget, *The Moral Judgment of the Child* (New York: Free Press, 1965), 120.
5. Goldman, Stein, and L'Engle, *Psychological Methods of Child Assessment.*
6. L. Bellak, *The TAT, the CAT and the SAT in Clinical Use* (New York: Grune & Stratten, 1975).
7. Ibid.; A. Rabin, ed., *Projective Techniques for Adolescents and Children* (New York: Springer, 1986).
8. Rabin, *Projective Techniques.*

9. W. Goodwin and L. Driscoll, *Handbook for Measurement and Evaluation in Early Childhood Education* (San Francisco: Jossey Bass, 1980).

10. Conte, "Prevention of Sexual Abuse."

11. "Preschool Child Abuse Efforts Seem Ineffective," *Los Angeles Times,* 24 February 1988, 3.

4
Parents' Participation: What Do They Learn?

alifornia's Child Abuse Prevention Training Act (CAPTA) was designed almost entirely for children. As written, the legislation specifies both the primacy of children as recipients of prevention monies and the curriculum content they are to receive. Secondarily, the legislation requires that parents and teachers receive prevention education and training. The parent training offers an orientation to the children's curriculum, which, in part, serves to appease parents' fears and concerns about their children's participation in the program. Beyond these sociopolitical functions, the meetings also present an opportunity to educate parents about child abuse and their role in its prevention.

The legislation requires that subjects covered in all parent meetings include the following:

> Information . . . delineating the problem and the range of possible solutions; workshops which are designed to help counteract common stereotypes about victims and offenders; information concerning physical and behavior indicators of abuse; crisis counseling techniques; community resources; rights and responsibilities regarding reporting; and caring for a child's needs after a report is made.[1]

While the subjects covered in most parent meetings are defined by the legislation, the meetings do not follow a rigid format. Rather, prevention programs are encouraged to use the parent meetings for individualized purposes, resulting in the diversity of some program emphases.

There were several reasons for analyzing the parent participation component of child abuse prevention training. Information about the children, their prior exposure to prevention concepts, and their familiarity with safety instruction delivered through the media could best be secured through parental accounts. Similarly, parents could be relied on to describe the safety precautions they use with their children as well as their perceptions of their children's safety skills. Most importantly, the study was designed to examine the impact of the parent meetings on parents' knowledge in the subject areas suggested for coverage in the legislation.

Research Design

The interview schedule for parents was designed to capture the basic content that the programs sought to convey. Some questions were open-ended so that parents could respond generally. Other questions were structured first to elicit parents' general responses and then to address a list of specific items to which they might respond.

Research staff were sensitive to the controversial nature of the subject of sexual abuse, particularly as it was being discussed in relation to children at an especially vulnerable age. While a few parents found the subject difficult to talk about, no parent terminated her or his interview. Since these parents were voluntary participants in the study, they may have been more predisposed to discuss the subject than would a random sample from the population at large.

Parent interviews for the pretest were usually conducted in person at the school at the parents' convenience. If an interview could not take place at school, the pretest was conducted over the phone. At the end of the interview parents were informed that they would be contacted again within two to three weeks to check in and discuss further some of the issues raised in the pretest. Posttests were conducted exclusively by telephone and took place within two to three weeks after the children's presentation. The need to obtain informed consent introduced an element of self-selection into the study sample. Parents who chose not to participate may have had very different characteristics than those who chose to participate.

The design of the study precluded the use of a control group. If significant pretest and posttest differences were found, the attribution of these differences to the parent meetings might be called into question in the absence of a control group. However, as very little change was actually demonstrated from pretest to posttest, the lack of a control group has little bearing on the internal validity of the findings.

Pretest and posttest parent interviews had different goals. At pretest, the instrument was designed to collect demographic data on the sample families. It also was important to explore how much current media coverage had affected parents or their children and what kinds of precautions and safety measures families followed. At posttest, we were interested in examining any knowledge gains that could be attributed to the parent meetings. In addition, posttest parent interviews were designed to elicit parents' perceptions of their children's behavior and knowledge in the area of child abuse.

Sample

One hundred sixteen parents participated in the pretest interview. In the posttest parents of children who had left school, had been reported for abuse, or otherwise had been dropped from the research were not reinterviewed. There was a 19 percent rate of attrition from the pretest, which left ninety-four parents in the final sample. Participating parents were primarily women (97 percent), mostly mothers and a few grandmothers and aunts. Many of the women interviewed were single mothers (31 percent).[2] Fathers participated in the study in 2 percent of the cases.

Race and income of participating families varied to some degree by school site. Thirty percent of participating parents were black, the majority from three project sites. Average family income for these sites was below $20,000 per year. The primary language spoken in the home was English for 93 percent of the families. Another 7 percent were bilingual, speaking English and Spanish. The mean age for mothers was thirty-three years with a range from twenty-one to forty-seven. The mean level of education for mothers was fourteen and a half years and for fathers fifteen years. Finally, parents had been in contact with the Department of Social Services in 12 percent of the cases, primarily through Aid to Families with Dependent Children (AFDC) payments to the family (see table 4–1).

Pretest Findings

Prior Exposure to Concepts

Parents were asked about the degree to which their child had been exposed to previous child abuse prevention concepts. Of the 116 parents interviewed for the pretest, 18 parents (16 percent) stated that their child had participated in a child abuse prevention workshop previously, usually through the child's preschool or day-care program. Thirty-two parents (26 percent) said that at least one other child in the family had some type of prevention training. Two-thirds of the children who had seen a prevention program had seen the CAP program; these children were primarily from sites receiving the CAPP and TSP curricula in this evaluation. Parents were unsure of the names of the programs their children had seen in other instances, or they referred to programs that were unfamiliar to the research staff. Of the children who had participated in workshops previously, most had participated approximately one year prior to the study. Two parents were unsure about when their child had last been trained.

A greater number of children had been exposed to prevention concepts through television viewing. Fifteen percent of the children had seen special programming sponsored by the "Romper Room" television show; 27 percent had seen child abuse prevention segments performed by the "Sesame Street" puppets; and 26 percent of all the children had seen public service announcements and commercials pertaining to abuse prevention. Children might have seen more than one type of television program. Combining all types of television viewing,

Table 4–1
Parent Sample

	Project							
	CAPP*	CSHP*	TSP*	TAT*	CAPIE*	YSAP*	SAFE*	Total
Number of parents pretested	16	16	15	17	19	15	18	116
Mean age of mother	33.8	35.1	38.8	31.0	25.4	31.4	29.4	32.2
Mean income (dollars)	10,000–20,000	20,000–30,000	40,000+	30,000–40,000	Under 10,000	Under 10,000	10,000–20,000	—
Language spoken	English (16)	English (14) Bilingual (1) Other (1)	English (14) Bilingual (1)	English (8) Bilingual (1) Unknown (8)	English (16) Unknown (3)	English (7) Bilingual (1) Other (1) Unknown (5)	English (14) Unknown (4)	English (89) Bilingual (5) Other (2) Unknown (20)
Prior contact with CPS	6	1	2	1	5	4	4	23
Marital status	SP† (12) DP† (1) Unknown (3)	SP (2) DP (14)	SP (2) DP (13)	SP (3) DP (6) Unknown (8)	SP (7) DP (9) Unknown (3)	SP (5) DP (2) Unknown (8)	SP (4) DP (10) Unknown (4)	SP (35) DP (55) Unknown (26)
Mean years of education	12.7	14.8	16.9	11.8	12.7	12.7	13.8	13.9
Ethnicity	100% B††	81% W†† 13% H†† 6% O††	94% W 6% A††	82% W 12% H 6% A	52% W 32% B 16% H	13% W 80% B 7% O	94% W 6% H	

Family Information Sheets returned	16	16	15	9	14	10	14	94
Number of parents posttested	16	16	12	11	9	14	16	94
Number of parents who attended parent meeting	10	10	5	2	6	2	4	39

*CAPP = Child Assault Prevention Project; CHSP = Children's Self-Help Project; TSP = Touch Safety Program; TAT = Talking About Touching; CAPIE = Child Abuse Prevention, Intervention and Education; YSAP = Youth Safety Awareness Project; SAFE = Stop Abuse through Family Education

†SP = sole parent; DP = dual parents

††B = black; W = white; H = Hispanic; O = other; A = Asian

61 percent of the sample children had seen some type of television show regarding the prevention of child abuse. Seventy percent of the parents felt that these shows and other types of media exposure had not affected their child in any way. Of those who felt the media had affected their child, the larger media issue relating to missing children was most frequently cited (13 percent). Parents next noticed that their children were more fearful of strangers (10 percent) or generally more worried (8 percent).

Safety Skills

Many parents teach their children safety skills at the preschool age by the frequent repetition of do's and don'ts. On pretest we asked parents about the kinds of do's and don'ts they teach their child. Perhaps because most parents understood that the nature of the study was related to abuse prevention, many did raise the subject of child abuse prevention when discussing the kinds of rules they talk about with their child. Parent's responses varied regarding do's and don'ts from:

"Don't run in the house or jump on the furniture."

"Don't run up the stairs."

"Don't talk with your mouth full."

to:

"If anyone touches you, tell Mom."

"I tell my son to tell people to leave the bathroom when he is using it. And if a teacher helps him undress, he should tell her to leave."

"Keep your dress down when you're playing."

"Don't kiss people on the mouth; let them kiss you on the cheek."

"People can't touch you, and if they do, be as obnoxious as you can. Yell."

The kinds of do's and don'ts that parents teach their children and the frequency with which parents mentioned certain kinds of rules by project site are reported in table 4–2. As the table shows, the most widely mentioned safety rule that parents teach their children deals with stranger danger. Beyond all other safety rules that might come to mind, parents seemed to be most concerned about teaching their children how to stay safe around strangers. This point is interesting for three reasons. First, when asked later in the interview how they believed their child would respond when confronted with strangers, most parents responded, "Well, my child would never meet a stranger without

Table 4–2
Parental Rules*

Project	Stranger Safety	Tell Parent	Say no	Child Abuse	Sexual Abuse	General Rules
CAPP†—Site A (n = 16)	12	4	2	3	5	6
CSHP†—Site B (n = 16)	11	2	1	5	3	9
TSP†—Site C (n = 15)	11	3	23	3	3	10
TAT†—Site D (n = 17)	14	1	0	4	3	2
CAPIE†—Site E (n = 19)	12	4	0	9	4	10
YSAP†—Site F (n = 15)	7	0	2	2	3	4
SAFE†—Site G (n = 18)	16	2	2	2	5	11
Total (n = 116)	83	16	9	28	26	52

*Parents were asked to respond spontaneously to this question: "Many parents have do's and don'ts that they teach their children. What are some of the do's and don'ts that you tell your child?" Responses were then coded by specific categories:

> Do's and don'ts related to stranger safety
> Do's and don'ts related to telling parents of uncomfortable situations
> Do's and don'ts related to saying no to others
> Do's and don'ts related to safety in generalized child abuse instances
> Do's and don'ts related to sexual abuse prevention
> General safety rules

The numbers in the table reflect affirmative responses from parents.
†CAPP = Child Assault Prevention Project; CSHP = Children's Self-Help Project; TSP = Touch Safety Program; TAT = Talking About Touching; CAPIE = Child Abuse Prevention, Intervention and Education; YSAP = Youth Safety Awareness Project; SAFE = Stop Abuse through Family Education

me" or "My child is never alone to encounter strangers by herself." Thus, while parents are highly concerned about their child's behavior around strangers, it is a situation the child rarely has an opportunity to experience. Second, while most instances of abuse and abduction are perpetrated by someone known to the child rather than by a stranger, parents still seem to cling to the notion of the bad stranger who will attempt to do harm to their child. This practice persists even though most parents indicated that they know that abuse by a family member or someone else known to the child is far more common than abuse by a stranger. Finally, as was noted in the discussion of the program impacts on children, the children's response on pretest and posttest indicated that parental admonitions seem to have a limited effect on stranger avoidance.

Rule Orientation

Because a number of the child abuse prevention programs focus on teaching children rules to follow under certain circumstances, parents were asked whether or not their child usually followed rules well. Given the age of the children studied, their general application of rules was quite positive. Many parents were confident that their child followed rules well, while only 15 percent stated that their child was not rule-oriented and had a good deal of trouble following rules.

Selection of Care Providers

How cautious are parents in selecting child-care services? Given the level of public concern surrounding child abuse and particularly around abuse perpetrated by a trusted care provider, it is important to assess the extent to which parents screen and evaluate service providers before entrusting their child to another's care. In this regard, 60 percent of the parents indicated that they made an informed choice, characterized by visits to the preschool, interviews with teachers and directors, conversations with parents already enrolled, and recommendations from trusted relatives or friends. Conversely, 13 percent of the parents stated that they had no choice in selecting a preschool; their children occupied limited state-funded slots in schools designated by the county. For remaining parents, the selection of their child's preschool seemed to be based mainly on convenience (for example, the school was located near the parent's home or place of employment, it was affordable, or its hours fit the parent's schedule).

Beyond the initial selection process, a few parents noted that they frequently arrived at the school unannounced to examine staff activities. In 47 percent of the cases, parents made regular visits to the school once a month or more either to help with school activities or to observe their child. Many parents made it a point to talk regularly with the teachers about school activities as well as their child's progress (54 percent), and almost all the parents spoke with their child daily about his or her school activities.

While there seemed to be a high level of screening related to day-care and preschool settings, the same rigor did not apply when choosing baby-sitters for children. One-half of the parents who used baby-sitters weekly did not screen their baby-sitters. The other 50 percent reported screening their baby-sitters with varying degrees of rigor.

To compare parents' overall sense of caution in leaving their child with other care providers, they were given composite scores combining six questions.[3]

Scores ranged from 3 to 24 with an ascending level of cautiousness. Figure 4–1 shows the distribution of scores. The even normal curve indicates that the majority of parents exercised a moderate level of caution with their child in a variety of situations.

Parental Predictions of Children's Behavior

Finally, parents were asked to make predictive judgments about their child's behavior in specific situations. Responses were then combined to look at parents' perceptions of their child's self-protective skills prior to the prevention training. Two questions showed a ceiling effect throughout the study sample on pretest, possibly indicating that prevention programs need not focus their attention on teaching children these particular skills. In the first question parents were asked whether their child knows a name or names for his or her private parts. Eighty-seven percent of the parents indicated that their child has a name, anatomical or slang, for the private parts of his or her body. The children who did not know the names were distributed fairly evenly across all sites; one site had a few more children in need of this information. In a second question parents were asked whether their child would yell or otherwise make a fuss if an adult attempted to grab him or her. Responses to this question also showed a high level of confidence at pretest. Eighty percent of the parents felt certain that their child would indeed yell. On a scale ranging from 6 to 18, parents described their children as highly self-protective on pretest.[4] Among the total sample of parents, the mean self-protective score for their children was 15.1.

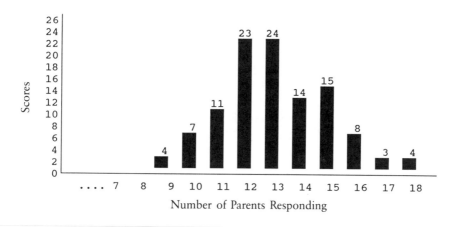

Figure 4–1. Distribution of Caution Scores

Posttest Findings

For a variety of reasons, one would anticipate a high level of participation in the parent component of child abuse prevention training programs for preschoolers. Due to their age, stature, developmental level, and impressionable disposition, these children are highly dependent on parents and caregivers. They require more supervision than older children, and they are more vulnerable to all types of harm. Thus, one would expect parents to observe the preschool environment in which their children spend time and to screen other care givers with prudence. The topic of sexual abuse is highly charged with emotional and intellectual implications for many parents. One might suppose that parents would be particularly selective regarding educational materials about sexual activities to which their preschool children might be exposed.

Attendance at Parent Meeting

How did parents respond to the opportunity for participation in the sexual abuse prevention training programs? Attendance at the parent meeting for each site was a strong indicator of parental interest in and concern about these programs. Here parents' questions could be addressed, parents could view much of the children's curriculum, and they could become better informed about the serious problem of child molestation. Parents in the seven study sites received letters about the site's parent meeting from the prevention program and were alerted to the subject both through the research study letter and the parent pretest interview. Many preschool teachers and administrators also strongly encouraged parents to attend this meeting. Interviews with prevention program administrators indicated that parents of preschool children were more responsive to the parent meeting than parents of older children.

In light of the above, the results of parents' attendance were somewhat surprising. Of 116 participating parents, 39 (34 percent) attended the parent meetings. Among those who did not attend, 6 percent stated that they had attended a meeting previously for another child in the family. At one school site, 43 percent of the parents stated that they had not been aware that such a meeting had taken place. (In actuality, this school's parents had been notified as were parents in other schools.) Others claimed an inability to attend due to a variety of factors, including scheduling, child care, and family illness.

The low rate of participation is even more remarkable when we consider that at three of the sites, participation at parent meetings is a general condition for a child's enrollment in the preschool program. At sites receiving the CAPP, YSAP, and SAFE curricula parents were expected to attend a given number of parent meetings throughout the course of the year. At the other sites parent meetings were regularly scheduled, although parent attendance was not required. Among the schools studied, attendance was relatively high at sites receiving CAPP and CSHP curricula, which were quite dissimilar in terms of demographic composition. Overall, the differential rates of parent participation cannot be adequately explained by the demographic data or the school requirements.

Another way to assess parental concern about child abuse prevention training is to consider the number who refuse their child's participation in programs of this nature across all communities. The state mandates that prevention programs be made available to all children but affords schools and parents the option of refusing the services. Before the programs are presented in the schools, permission slips are sent home with children to solicit parental approval. The permission slips are written so that parents who disapprove of their children's participation must return the slip to the schools. Very few of these permission slips are ever returned to the schools, and thus most children participate. This procedure of passive approval is difficult to interpret. It may indicate that parents generally approve of the programs. It also may reflect the extent to which children forget or lose letters intended for their parents, the extent to which parents read and respond to messages their children bring home, or the prevalence of non–English speaking parents who do not understand the contents of these letters when written in English.

Parental Acceptance of Prevention Programs

To gain a better sense of parents' attitudes toward their children's prevention programs than might be gleaned from the passive approval of unreturned permission slips, several questions on this issue were explored. Specifically, parents were asked if they had felt adequately informed about the content of the children's workshop, if they had experienced any concerns about their child's participation, and if they had felt any pressure to have their child participate in the workshops. The answers to all these questions gave strong indications that the parents had very few reservations about the workshops. Only 20 percent of the parents did not feel well informed about the content and purpose of the children's presentation. About half of these parents came from one school site. Other parents in the study sample who did not feel adequately informed were evenly dispersed among the school sites. Many of these parents had confused the research project workshops with the prevention program, revealing a high degree of uncertainty about the purpose of the program itself.

Few parents noted misgivings about the workshops. Only 8 percent of all parents expressed concern about their child's participation. The proportion was somewhat higher (15 percent) among those who attended the parent meetings, although they ultimately granted their child's participation. Two percent of all parents felt pressured to have their child participate.

Indicators of such strong support and positive regard for the prevention programs must be tempered with a thought to the population sample. In each of the study sites there may have been parents who did not consent to participate in the study because they had negative attitudes and concerns about the prevention program, which led them to resist getting involved in our study. In the same vein, willing participants in the research may have had a certain propensity toward acceptance of the prevention program's methods.

Parents not only showed high regard for the programs, but also indicated great reliance on the programs to teach their children specific safety skills. Indeed, there was a significant increase in the parents' perception of their children's self-protection skills from a pretest mean score of 15.1 to a posttest of 16.2 ($t = 5.81$, $p < .001$) following participation in the program (see endnote 4).

Prevalence of Child Sexual Abuse

On the substantive content of the parent meetings, a few central concepts taught by all the prevention programs were examined to assess the impact of the component of parent attitudes, perceptions, and knowledge. First, we compared parents' perceptions of the prevalence of child abuse. Exact figures on the rate of abuse are not available, but the median rate estimated across several studies reports 20 percent of females and 7 percent of males are sexually abused in childhood.[5]

Responses on pretest regarding the prevalence of child sexual abuse indicated that 28 percent of the parents believed that 25 to 49 percent of children are sexually abused. There was very little difference between the pretest sample of those who attended the parent meetings and the total sample. A surprising number of parents believed the problem of child sexual abuse to be even more widespread. Twenty-nine percent of the parents stated that 50 to 100 percent of all children in the United States are victimized in childhood.

The parent meetings did little to change parents' perceptions of the rate of abuse. On posttest, 38 percent of the parents reported prevalence rates between 25 and 49 percent (the increase was not significant). Yet a full 25 percent of the parents still clung to the belief that most children are sexually abused (see figure 4–2).

Perpetrators of Sexual Abuse

On pretest almost half the sample (42 percent) stated that 75 to 100 percent of offenders are not strangers. Little difference was demonstrated on posttest, as 46 percent of the parents reported that most children are abused by someone they know. Although parents' knowledge about offenders is quite accurate, it is interesting that they exhibit an overarching fear of strangers with regard to their children's safety (see figure 4–3).

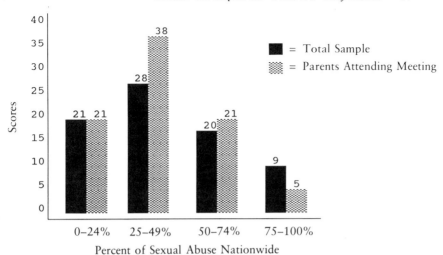

Figure 4–2. Parent Perceptions of Abuse Rates Nationwide

Indicators of Abuse

While the exact rate of sexual abuse is unknown, it is clear that sexual abuse is a crime most often committed by someone known to the child. Thus parents' responses were reasonably accurate in regard to this general question. Because the perpetrator is often known to the victim, this issue compounds an already difficult circumstance. The power imbalance between the child victim and the offender is quite obvious. Also, children are often made to feel that the abuse is their own fault. Due to these factors and others, young children are frequently reluctant to tell anyone about the abuse, although they often give clues to the abuse through their behavior. Some of the typical signs of abuse include a sudden and unexplained change in the child's sleeping patterns—nightmares and bed-wetting—or a change in the child's eating patterns—either ceasing to eat or eating compulsively. Behavioral indicators of abuse do not follow a set pattern, nor do all children display the same kinds of behaviors. Yet because watching for and noticing a dramatic change in a child's behavior may be one of the only ways that parents can identify the problem, it is important that parents are aware of possible signs of abuse.

Program presenters at the parent meetings discussed signs that parents might look for in an abused child. Seeking to tap parents' knowledge about physical and behavioral signs of abuse on both the pretest and posttest, we asked parents, "What might make you think a child had been sexually abused?" In coding responses to this question, we gave parents a score based on the number of indicators they mentioned. The literature suggests at least ten symptoms that

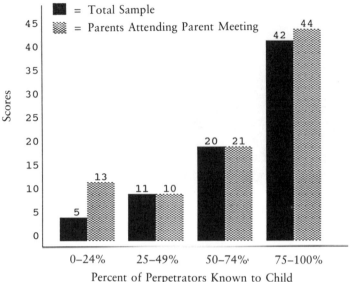

Figure 4–3. Parent Perceptions of Perpetrators

might indicate to parents that a child had been sexually abused.[6] The assumption here was that the more physical and behavioral indicators parents recognized as possibly related to abuse, the better equipped they might be to notice these signs. The results, however, show very few indicators mentioned by parents and no significant change in the number of indicators parents said they might recognize before and after the parent meetings. On pretest those attending the parent meetings attained a mean score of 1.85, which increased very slightly on posttest to 1.97 ($t = .70, p = .491$). The pretest score for the group that did not attend the parent meetings was 1.89.[7]

Parents occasionally referred to one generalized change in their child's behavior that they might recognize as an indicator of abuse—for example, "I'd just know by the way he acts" or "She'd just act different, but I would know." Often the behavior change was reported as primarily affective, with abused children described as withdrawn, passive, quiet, or timid. A handful of parents who were well versed in the subject noted a variety of signs, including urinary tract infections, vaginal bleeding, or reenacting the scene in their play or with dolls. A surprising number of parents, however, were confident that their recognition of abuse would be immediate and intuitive. Comments such as "I'd see it in her eyes and just know" arose in both the pretest and posttest, even though the information delivered at the parent meetings contradicted the fact that parents would just know. Of course, many parents can intuitively recognize when their child is or is not feeling well, and it is possible that the first step toward identifying abuse might be an intuitive one for parents. Yet the prevention programs emphasize the importance of identifying specific behavioral signs of abuse and seek to move parental recognition of abusive circumstances beyond the level of intuition.

Reporting Abuse

In addition to the indicators that might help to identify abused children, the meetings also focused on what parents can do once abuse has been detected. Unlike many professionals who work with children, parents are not mandated in California to report abuse should they have cause to be suspicious. Parent meetings, however, stress the importance of reporting abuse as a means of protecting the child. To elicit the type of reporting action parents might take, the parents were asked, "If one of your child's playmates told you s/he had been abused by a stranger, what do you think you would do?" This question was asked on both pretest and posttest for parents who attended the parent meetings and on pretest alone for those who did not attend. Responses were scored on a scale of 0 to 2 depending on whether parents mentioned the police or children's protective services (cps) as agencies to whom they would report. The parents' mean score on pretest was .21, increasing slightly to .41 on posttest ($t = 1.75, p = .088$).

Parents were then asked to differentiate their response depending on whether the abuse had been committed by a stranger or by the child's parent. Given that hypothetical situation, parents showed very little differentiation in their responses after the parent meeting. On pretest, parents had a mean score of .54, which increased to .69 on posttest ($t = 1.43, p = .160$).

The disparity between parents' scores for the two hypothetical conditions indicates that parents made differential responses depending on the perpetrator of the abuse. The difference on pretest between the actions parents might take if they discovered abuse by a stranger as opposed to abuse by the child's parent was highly significant ($t = 3.35, p = .002$) and remained so on posttest ($t = 2.91, p = .006$). While respondents appeared more likely to make a report to public authorities if they were suspicious of abuse by a child's parent, reporting scores for both hypothetical situations were low, and in most instances many parents did not know to call either the police or cps.

Looking at the other responses parents suggested in answer to the above stated question, we found that in the majority of cases the parents felt that the most appropriate response to an abused child would be to handle such a matter privately, through the child's parents, rather than to move through a public agency to address the problem. On pretest 54 percent of the parents in the study sample felt that if the offender were a stranger, they would talk with the child's parents about the problem. In those instances where the abuse was within the child's family, it was far more likely that the parents would turn to cps (33 percent), to the police (25 percent), or to the child's teacher (16 percent to report the issue. Ten percent still felt, however, that the problem would best be handled by talking with the abusing parent or his or her spouse.

The findings with respect to this issue were not dramatically different among the sample of parents who attended the parent meetings. On pretest, 51 percent of the parents said that they would turn to the child's parents if a child were abused by a stranger. If the parent were the offender, 13 percent of the parents still relied on the alleged offender or the offender's spouse as a potential helper in the situation. On posttest, 46 percent of the parents said that they would talk with the child's parents in an instance of abuse by a stranger. And even after attending the parent meetings, 13 percent of the parents still felt inclined to call on the abuser or his or her spouse to redress the situation. (For a more detailed description of responses to these questions, see figures 4–4 and 4–5.)

When parents were initially asked how they would respond to the disclosure of child abuse, many could not offer specific actions, expressing instead comments such as the following:

"I don't know. I'd be shocked."

"I'd be upset, but I'd try not to show how upset I'd be."

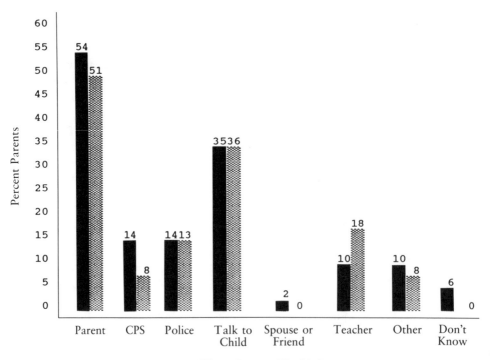

Figure 4–4. Reporting Stranger Abuse: Parent Responses

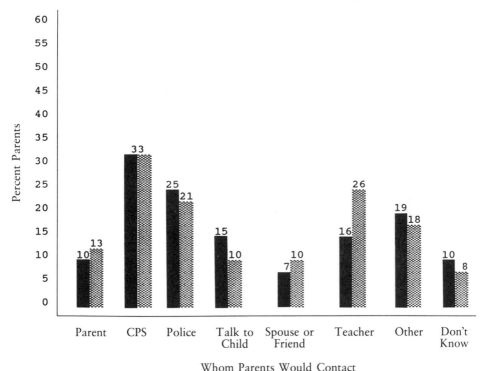

Figure 4–5. Reporting Parental Abuse: Parent Responses

"It's a scary thought. It's wrong. It's sick. Especially with relatives."

"It's tough to know."

In contrast, a few parents offered specific actions that were rather extreme:

"You really want to know? I'd kill 'em. I have no regard for anyone who does this to a child. I'd get the person out. Get a restraining order."

"I'd go after any abuser. Child abuse should be grounds for the death penalty."

Some parents showed sympathy for the child who might be abused, but they added in their comments:

"I'd never let my child play with that kid again."

"I'd make the little friend comfortable but then would tell my daughter not to play with the little friend anymore or go play at the friend's house."

From these parents there was an air of contagion regarding the problem, as though their own child might catch the abuse from the other child.

Finally, a number of parents spoke of their skepticism concerning a child's story of abuse and stated that they would talk with the child to discern the validity of the accusation. These parents questioned the possibility that children might not tell the truth. Comments such as "I'd see if it's a fantasy" or "I don't want an innocent person to get in trouble" attest to some parents' suspicion about disclosures they might receive from children, especially if the offender was a relative of the child.

Summary: Parent Involvement and Views

According to the parents, more than half the children had seen one or more television messages regarding safety issues, stranger danger, or touching, although very few of the children had ever received any formal training in their preschools. While parents taught their children a variety of safety rules, the focus of their instruction was on stranger wariness.

The degree of caution parents exercised when leaving their children in the hands of others varied, with more care taken in selecting formal child-care providers than in choosing baby-sitters. Perhaps because of the highly publicized reports of abuse in day-care and preschool centers, parents were more wary of these caretakers than others.

Parents did not show a particular aversion to their children's exposure to prevention training. Whether or not the children had actually learned the concepts presented, parents felt that their children were safer after participation in the programs.

The component of the study designed solely for parents did not appear particularly useful. Parents demonstrated an extremely low rate of attendance at parent meetings and showed little or no knowledge gains in four significant areas.

Given the results from the parent component of the study, a thorough examination of recruitment methods and program content of parent education meetings is indicated. Parent meetings, as currently conducted, may serve to acquaint some parents with their children's curricula but seem to do little in the way of educating them about child abuse. The low rate of parent participation further calls into question whether these results justify program expenditures on the component in its current form. If parent participation is deemed a desirable element of prevention training, more rigorous efforts are required to engage and educate this group.

Notes

1. Welfare and Institutions Code, Section 18953.3, Assembly Bill No. 2443, Chapter 1638, Article 2.

2. The percentage of single female–headed households for 1983 was 36 percent nationally (U.S. Department of Commerce, Bureau of the Census, Current Population Report, Series P. 60, No. 145). While California figures may be somewhat different, these figures may imply a close correlation between the sample population in the study and the total state population of female-headed households.

3. The questions in the scale are:
   a. Do you use babysitters?
   b. How often do you use babysitters?
   c. Is there anything you do to screen [babysitters]?
   d. How often do you generally talk with your child about what he/she does at preschool?
   e. How often do you generally talk with your child's teacher about what [child's name] does at preschool?
   f. How many times in the last 6 months have you visited your child's preschool?

4. The questions in the scale are:
   a. Do you think your child would tell you if an adult attempted to touch him/her in a way that made her/him feel uncomfortable?
   b. Do you think your child would think it was his/her fault if he/she were abused?
   c. Does your child know the names of his/her private parts?
   d. If a stranger approached your child, would your child stay out of the stranger's arms reach?
   e Would your child yell or otherwise make a fuss if an adult attempted to grab him or her?
   f. Do you think your child would know the difference between a touch that was potentially sexually abusive and one that was not?

5. David Finkelhor and Associates (eds.), *A Sourcebook on Child Sexual Abuse* (Beverly Hills: Sage Publications, 1986).

6. Richard S. Riggs, "Incest: The School's Role," *The Journal of School Health* 52, no. 8 (August 1982): 367.

7. Parents who did not attend the meetings were not asked this question on post-test. It was assumed that their responses would be similar.

5
Teachers and Social Workers: Views on Prevention Programs

The main focus of the research project was to examine the impact of prevention programs on children and their parents. However, research staff were also interested in how teachers and preschool administrators reacted to the prevention program, as well as how the prevention program affected the larger system of children's protective services (cps). To answer these questions, preschool administrators were interviewed prior to the prevention program, teachers were asked for their comments following the in-class presentation, and cps officials in the corresponding counties were interviewed after research staff completed posttesting at the school sites.

Impacts on Preschool Administration

To what extent did growing public attention on child abuse affect the policies and practices of preschool administrators? Research staff were particularly interested in discerning whether the increased media attention and public awareness of child abuse had changed any of the daily practices in child-care settings. Of the seven preschool administrators interviewed, only one felt confident that nothing had changed at the school site since the increased attention to and awareness of child abuse had emerged. The director at this school stated that she and her staff did not feel the least vulnerable: "The setting is so open, so concerned about kids' safety, and so closely supervised by parents and staff that there's no reason to be concerned." In contrast to some of the other school sites, this school had a very high degree of parent participation as part of its daily routine.

Other administrators felt that changes had occurred over the past few years. One school in particular had become far more aware of the concerns surrounding child abuse in day-care settings and had instituted specific procedures to protect both its children and its teachers. For example, in an effort to lessen the vulnerability of the teachers to false accusations, one-on-one teacher–child activities had been cut to a minimum, and a team approach to child supervision had been adopted in the school.

While some of the school administrators had not sensed a change in their staffs' interactions with the children, others had initiated policy changes that would require taking a different approach to working with the children. Primarily in those activities that centered on toileting, changing clothes, and napping, administrators had instituted tighter operating rules. Where teachers had once assisted children alone, they were now required to leave the door open and to assist children only in the company of other teachers.

Staff practices regarding physical affection with the children had not changed directly. Some administrators discussed the homelike environment of their schools and the importance of physical affection with this age group. One director also stressed the importance of maintaining good touches with the children. All the administrators, however, reported that their staffs were more conscientious and aware than they had been previously.

Three schools had men on their teaching staffs, yet only one administrator noticed the man's greater degree of caution with the children. Here, the male staff member was more cautious in his demonstration of affection but was primarily concerned about toileting habits and made sure that a woman was present at all times when he was assisting a child. While most other administrators stated that they would not actively discriminate in their hiring practices against a male applicant, one administrator stated that she would be unable to hire a man due to the school owner's wishes.

Administrators also were asked whether they had noticed more concern among parents about the issue of child abuse in day care. While directors universally reported parents' growing concern about child abuse, most felt that parents saw the preschool as a supportive environment in which to talk about the issue. Guided by parents' requests, parent meetings were organized to discuss topics of physical and sexual child abuse. Directors also sought to involve parents as much as possible in the activities of the schools, from policy development to aiding in the classroom. Mothers were cited as more involved in school meetings and activities, although fathers were said to be more involved recently than in years past.

To gain a greater sense of how frequently school sites were monitored or observed from the outside, we asked administrators about whether they encouraged parents to drop in at the school and whether parents felt as though they were welcome to do so. All administrators indicated positive responses, stating that parents generally knew that they were welcome any time.[1] Directors also were asked about visits from the state's Licensing Department. While these visits are often unannounced, they are part of a system of external control and supervision over an often semiprivate environment. It was reported that officials from the Licensing Department had made visits to all of the schools at least once in the past two years. One school whose license was being reviewed for renewal had had six inspections over the past year.

Directors were asked whether they or anyone on their staffs had ever made a child abuse report. All the directors except two indicated that they had made reports. One noted that while she had not made a report, she was "on the verge" of doing so. The directors' experiences with cps were quite positive in most instances, with more rapid service being reported for younger than for older children. Children who had been reported were said to have been well handled by cps officials, although all the administrators mentioned the parents as most problematic and most disturbed by the school's report. In some cases parents were so upset by the teacher's or director's report that they removed their child from the school.

Impacts on Teacher Actions and Behavior

While classroom teachers were not interviewed prior to the presentation of the program, their input after the presentation was very useful in understanding the context of the prevention program within the classroom environment. Teachers were asked to discuss their impressions of the children's training as well as the usefulness of the teacher training sponsored by the prevention agency.

When asked about the value of the teacher training, most teachers saw it as generally positive. Many stated that they had a great number of concerns before the program, which were addressed by the workshop leaders. One enthusiastic teacher noted, "It gave facts that were pretty impressive. I didn't know there was so much abuse, but it really sunk in. It made an impression that it's really useful to teach this for this age group."

Most teachers stated that the training helped them to know what to expect in the children's workshop or that it refreshed their memory about the issue. In most cases teachers felt more comfortable with the subject and better able to deal with parents' questions about the program and issues of child abuse.

Some assessments were less favorable. Teachers from one school site expressed considerable disappointment with the teacher presentation and were quite dismayed with the children's program. As one teacher put it, "There was no program. We had no idea what to expect." Other teachers also expressed mixed emotions about the children's program. While teachers saw a certain level of usefulness for programs aimed at four- and five-year-olds, many had concerns about training for three-year-olds. Mirroring the concerns expressed by the parents, teachers at one school site had a number of reservations about the program. One teacher stated, "The program may not be age appropriate in the way it's presented. The skits are too explicit and too advanced for their needs."

The classroom teacher who served as the prevention trainer reported, "I put pressure on myself. It didn't come from anyone else. Even with the confidence

I have with kids and talking with kids I really had to think about it a lot before I began." When asked whether or not she felt the workshop was useful to the children in her classroom, this teacher answered in the affirmative, noting:

> The day of the first lesson I asked them who keeps them safe. They named *everybody* except for themselves. Since then they've really learned that they have a lot to do with it, too. We hug ourselves, we do role plays, and I get them to make their own decisions.

Teachers at another school site perceived a similar impact of the program on their children. They felt that the children had a better sense of their "personal safety" and that they were more "responsible for themselves."

Teachers were asked what the children had talked about most after the program. At one school site children were reported as more assertive after the program: They were saying no more frequently, stating that they were "safe, strong, and free," and, up to a week following the program, they were assertively responding to teachers with comments such as "I have a right to talk." Teachers from other sites also noticed children repeating words and songs from the prevention program and had heard children mentioning "red light" touches or singing the "red light" song quite frequently. The teachers stated that they also used this terminology with their students.

One of the implicit goals of the children's programs is to encourage disclosures of abuse and to establish a safe atmosphere in which children feel comfortable talking with the presenters or their teacher. Following the children's training sessions, however, no immediate disclosures were made to presenters or preschool staff, and two months later disclosures were still virtually absent. According to program providers, this experience is typical, as they generally meet with very few disclosures from children at the preschool level.

Following the presentation teachers were asked to describe the children's initial reactions to the material and what the children were most responsive to during the presentation. The programs that employed puppets to convey their ideas were most successful in capturing the children's attention. Attitudes were mixed, however, regarding the puppets' usefulness in actually delivering the program's message. Although children were said to be attentive, one teacher felt that the content was lost, as the puppets and other props were more a distraction than a point of focus. Similarly, teachers at a second site felt that while the children enjoyed watching the puppets, they were hesitant to actively interact with them.

In response to the question of whether teachers might have felt bothered or uncomfortable with any aspects of the training, responses varied considerably. At four of the school sites no concerns were voiced about the program's presentation. Among respondents who did express concern, at one site it was based more on the presentation than the content: "Two women presented. I felt it was hard for the children to imagine the women being men or children (in the role plays)." Similarly, comments from other sites were critical about the manner of presentation rather than the concepts of the program: "We still had strong reservations about the skits, especially. Kids at that age aren't ready for that kind of information; kids may not be able to integrate that kind of information."

These teachers felt strongly about helping children to learn certain skills (say no, run away, and tell) and were impressed with the program's ability to convey these skills. Their concerns, however, focused on the mode of presentation. One teacher expressed the concerns of the school staff and parents when she said, "The incest scene was very difficult to watch. Parents have the most trouble with this scene because they don't want Dad to be made out as a bad or mistrustful figure for kids."

Finally, there was some criticism about the program's concepts. One teacher observed: "We try not to have tattlers at school; to have them yell and tell someone is not always appropriate." Teachers from this school also offered constructive advice on how to work more appropriately with the younger children: "for three- and four-year-olds, simplify the examples of strangers and bribes and only use red and green lights. The yellow light is too sophisticated. Besides, a yellow light can't change to green, it can only turn red."

Teacher observations about the presenters' level of expertise were almost universally positive. They found the presenters dedicated, conscientious, and very comfortable with the children. Better classroom management could have been demonstrated in some instances, but otherwise presentations were judged as well done.

At the conclusion of the interview teachers were asked if they felt these programs should be required in all preschools. Again, opinions varied by school site and by teacher. Few teachers thought the programs should be mandatory, while more thought the curricula should be available in all schools. Most teachers felt that the curriculum they received should be modified somwhat but still presented: "I believe in what they're presenting, just not in how they do it"; "the meaning of the curriculum should be presented." Teachers at several schools thought that the curriculum at their school was fine for four- or five-year-olds but not appropriate for three-year-olds or younger. Finally, teachers at two school sites stressed that the material needed to be "Just like fire drills, learning how to keep yourself safe," adding that the schools may be able to provide the material themselves "if they would take the time."

Impacts on Children's Protective Services

Interviews were conducted with administrators in six of the seven counties studied. In the seventh county, an interview was conducted with an official from the Department of Public Health. The purpose of these interviews was to gain some insight into the impact child abuse prevention training may have had on cps agencies. Had the number of reports increased or decreased over the past few years? Could any change be attributed to prevention programs? How did cps officials view the prevention programs?

With one exception, all county cps officials stated that their counties had experienced an increase in child abuse reports over the past five years, some increasing by more than 25 percent. In the county where a decrease was noted, the cps administrator suggested that this trend "may be due to the prevention programs or it may be because of better screening by the workers."

How much of the general increase in child abuse reporting might be attributed directly to the prevention programs? At this point, data management within the cps system does not identify the agency or the professional who makes a report. As cps becomes more sophisticated in data management, it will no doubt account for the origin of a call as well as its destination. Such tracking would be useful in helping to demonstrate the number of reports generated by prevention programs and whether those reports were better substantiated or more thoroughly grounded than reports from other agencies or individuals. Under the present system, the information on this topic is mainly anecdotal and impressionistic.

Of the seven public officials interviewed, five felt certain that the trend toward increased reporting would continue. In the words of one official, "The numbers will probably continue to go up. Programs are teaching children to disclose. Some kids are learning how to protect themselves, but most are just learning to tell." Other officials believed that, through greater public awareness and stronger school personnel training, reports might occur at an earlier stage in the abuse and that they would be better substantiated when investigated. One official disagreed, noting that "the community knows we're not in the business of primary prevention." She thought that reports are unlikely to be made at an earlier stage because community members do not expect cps to take action before the problem is clear and serious.

Finally, some counties seem to have strong, well-established relationships with their prevention agencies. These counties actively engage in regular meetings with prevention program staff, they act as a backup to one another at parent and teacher meetings, and they communicate well with one another regarding cases reported by the prevention agency. In counties where the prevention agency's relationship with cps is not as well established, problems were identified by cps officials as resting both within the prevention agency and within cps. One cps administrator openly admitted that the strain in his county exists because of a "clogged system" within cps. Here the cps hot line available for incoming calls is not sufficient for the number of reports received, and prevention workers and other professionals often have to wait up to forty-five minutes for their report to be taken. In another county, the cps administrator said that the relationship with the prevention agency was rocky: "They're probably critical of our inaccessibility, but they (the prevention agency reports) tend to be more unfounded and unsubstantiated." Finally, one cps administrator was very critical of the prevention agency in his community. He claimed, "They are saturating the market for reporters. There are too many reports that aren't accurate or appropriate—especially the claims on sexual abuse."

Summary

Media coverage surrounding child abuse seems to have had an impact on many preschool and day-care settings. Routine child supervision, bathroom supervision, and napping arrangements have been altered. Similarly, while many teachers report that their practices have not changed, they often give more thought to expressing affection with children than they did in earlier years, and many describe this change with regret.

Teachers generally found the teacher training to be useful, and many supported the children's training as well. Concerns were voiced, however, about the presentation of the preschool curriculum to children under the age of four, and some teachers were critical of the presentations.

General impressions from cps departments show some weaknesses in their data management systems. Ill-defined categories and poor data collection techniques do not allow social service agencies to track founded, unfounded, and unsubstantiated reports of child abuse. Most counties do not have the means to locate the originator of child abuse reports and thus can give only impressionistic accounts of the impact of prevention programs on the generation of child abuse reports. Information from teachers and program providers suggests that the classroom training did not have a perceptible impact on disclosures by preschool children.

Note

1. It was later gleaned from parents at one school site that while visits were welcomed by the school administrators, parents had been clearly informed that visits could take place only on a scheduled basis to decrease program interruption.

6
Preschool Development: What Can Children Learn?

T his chapter examines the developmental attributes of preschool children between the ages of three and one-half and five years. It addresses several questions regarding what children of this age can learn and how they can learn in light of developmental theory. These questions ask: Is the content of prevention programs developmentally appropriate for young children? Are some concepts or lessons more salient to preschool needs and understanding than others? Are the methods of presenting program materials developmentally appropriate for young children?

Developmental Profile

Child development occurs within several domains. The domains to be covered in this chapter include cognitive, moral, and psychosocial. Child development is usually an asynchronistic process, as a child's progress in one domain may be more rapid than it is in another.[1] Further, each child has her[2] own developmental pace, which may differ from those of others of her cohort. Perhaps the most important factor to keep in mind when considering developmental stages and achievements is that they occur sequentially and hierarchically, with one building on another.[3] While the stages are conceptually distinct, in the developmental process there is often an overlap. The transition between stages is gradual and can be quite lengthy.

Cognitive Development

Cognitive theory focuses primarily on the development of thinking or cognition, initially in relation to the inanimate world.[4] Its influence on and relationship to affective and social growth is a recent integration of several theoretical dimensions.[5] Both these aspects of cognitive development have a bearing on the subject at hand.

In Piagetian terms, preschool childen are in the preoperational stage of development. They have completed the sensory-motor stage in which learning, exploration, and expression all occur on an active, physical level and now increasingly rely on language—both expressive and receptive.[6]

The preoperational child can mentally manipulate only one conceptual dimension at a time.[7] She does not perceive two characteristics simultaneously, nor can she allow additional experience to modify her initial perception. Rather the young child will concentrate either on the quality or quantity of an object as it is immediately observed.[8] As we will show, this limited ability to grasp multidimensional concepts has direct implications for the preschooler's comprehension of the most basic ideas in child abuse prevention curricula.

For the young child logic and understanding are closely correlated to the exact context in which an idea is introduced.[9] She is most apt to grasp ideas conveyed in familiar terms or set in familiar settings. Conversely, abstract concepts or those that differ from the concepts to which the child is accustomed present cognitive challenges beyond many children's ability to understand.[10]

The thinking of the preschool child has been characterized as egocentric. Visually, she "cannot anticipate how an object will look from another point of view or even realize that it will look any different."[11] It has been posited that this approach to perceptual knowledge is extended beyond the visual to the social. Within this theoretical framework the child assumes that everyone thinks as she does and understands the world in much the same way. The child's empathic abilities develop, albeit slowly, during this period.[12] Her emotional responses to certain situations also are generalized to the universal since the child imagines that everyone feels as she does.

While this egocentric characteristic has been traditionally described by Piaget and his followers, more recent work in this area indicates that young children are capable of taking the viewpoint of another if it is in some way consistent with their experience, indicating again that concepts must be presented within a familiar context.[13] The younger preschooler can take other visual perspectives, but the gradual inclusion of the ability to recognize the differing feelings and intentions of others is not achieved until later in a child's preschool years.[14]

In the process of developing an awareness of her world and an understanding of her experiences, the preschooler gradually begins to perceive the symbolic representation of objects and actions.[15] The child engages in make-believe and symbolic play. Toys, objects, and materials often are used symbolically rather than literally, with a cup serving alternately as a boat, a shovel, and a hat. The child becomes the other, acting out the roles of people, animals, and fantasy characters. This has a clear connection to the child's cognitive development, for in internalizing observations and experiences through symbolic play, she is simultaneously assimilating them.

Moral Development

The preschool child's moral development occurs along lines similar to those of cognitive development, following stages that are sequential, hierarchical, and structural.[16] Much of the work in the moral domain has focused on children six and over Piaget notes, "[W]e were unable to question children under 6 with any profit because of the intellectual difficulties of comparison."[17] Kohlberg, however, did some work with four- and five-year-olds and found both differences and similarities between his findings and those of Piaget.[18]

A child's chronological age is an important point of reference when speaking of development. But in the development process, the essential factor is that a child must complete any given stage before moving on to the next, with secondary interest placed on the age at which this is accomplished. With this in mind, we will assume that Piaget's and Kohlberg's initial stages of development are applicable to preschoolers. Since some of the research on which these theories are based was done with children slightly older than those in our sample, however, this assumption should be viewed with caution. It may be that the children in this study, especially the younger ones, are in an earlier stage not yet described.

It should be noted that Kohlberg bases his theory on work conducted cross-culturally in a multitude of settings. Since Kohlberg's findings at many points dovetail with Piaget's, this cross-cultural dimension lends further support to Piaget's work, which has been criticized for including only white working-class boys.[19] The initial stage as posited by both Piaget and Kohlberg (and the one that applies to the preschool child) is typified by reliance on external standards or qualities. This stage is referred to as one of heteronomous morality,[20] wherein the child's unquestioning deference toward adult authority—especially adults upon whom she depends—is paramount. According to Kohlberg, the preschool child's concern is that of obedience in order to avoid punishment.

Further, the young child has not yet formulated an internal autonomous conscience that allows one to judge the merit of individual acts. Her concrete cognitive structures are reflected in the fact that the preschool child tends to be absolutist in her thinking, favoring clear and definite categories and eschewing the ambiguous.[21] Visible, definable, concrete characteristics such as sex, color, or quantity are cited by the preschooler as rationales for meting out justice. For example, in Piaget's classic example of a child who broke one object under circumstances that adults would generally consider naughty and another child who broke multiple objects under accidental circumstances, the youngest children in his study considered the quantity of damage as more important than the underlying motive in judging the misconduct attributable to these acts. Piaget refers to this phenomenon as objective responsibility in which the child ascribes all responsibility to external elements.[22] Thus, for the preschool child, reliance on outside individuals or factors is a salient element in moral judgment. This view fits with Kohlberg's first stage of moral development, in which rules are understood in relation to the consequences of punishment by an authority figure.

The theories of Piaget and Kohlberg are not without competition. Social learning theory, for example, critiques the premises of cognitive-structural theory,[23] thus displacing a system that is sequential and hierarchical. Bandura has shown that "children's judgmental responses are readily modifiable, particularly through the utilization of adult modeling cues."[24] His theory proposes that stages can be accelerated or even reversed through modeling the behavior of others. After children's exposure to an adult's moral reasoning, children have been shown to respond particularly well to reasoning based in the moral stage directly above their own. These effects have been tested for retention up to a two-week period.[25] However, the work in this area has been carried out primarily with latency age children and adolescents, while little work has been completed with very young children.

Moral and Conventional Transgressions

Recently, a number of studies have been undertaken to identify the extent to which an emerging sense of morality is dependent on cognitive development (from preoperational to concrete operations). Damon's study, for example, associates children's reasoning about justice with their logical reasoning based on concrete operations.[26] Piaget's theory of heteronomous morality also has been challenged, as studies have shown that relations between children and authority figures are actually multidimensional and dependent on the environmental context.[27]

From another perspective on the concept of moral development, it has been suggested that as young as the preschool years, children make distinctions between true moral transgressions and conventional morality, defined by societal arrangement.[28] Moral transgressions are categorized according to the intrinsic consequences of an action, particularly one that inflicts harm or pain on people.[29] Conventional matters are based on social standards of practice (for example, manners or a dress code). Regardless of children's age, studies report that most subjects view moral transgressions negatively. Activities found in the conventional domain of morality are viewed with greater variation.[30] Under circumstances of conventional justice, children's perceptions of the immorality of an action are based on social rules or norms that might prohibit the act. In fact, Smetana shows that in the eyes of the preschooler, conventional transgressions are more permissible in the absence of a rule and that rules are the defining boundaries for such events.[31] These studies indicate that if the child perceives the event as a true moral transgression, she will be more likely to understand the event as wrong and may be more likely to state her concerns about the action. But if she views the event in terms of a social construct, that child will be more easily persuaded to abandon the rule when placed in a different setting or when given equally persuasive arguments for its acceptability.

Psychosocial Development

By the time a child reaches preschool age, she has completed several early stages of psychosocial development. The first stage addresses her emotional and physical needs and introduces her initial need to satisfy her desire for security, comfort, and protection. This stage is called variously attachment,[32] symbiosis,[33] and trust versus mistrust.[34] It has certain discernible commonalities that can be ascertained cross-culturally.[35] Optimum development and completion of this stage is dependent on satisfactorily establishing a viable attachment to at least one nurturing figure upon whom the child can depend—an individual she can trust and with whom physical closeness develops into eventual emotional closeness and subsequent ego development. With the successful completion of this initial stage, the child begins to make tentative movements toward individuation: the development of the self as an individual separate from the attachment figure. This stage has many constructive, development-enhancing attributes and is an inherent aspect of individual growth.[36] Exploration of the environment, both animate and inanimate, is an integral part of this stage of the separation–individuation process during which the child strives to develop a sense of autonomy and selfhood.[37]

The quest for autonomy can be rife with conflict for the child. She requires firm outer controls to guide her through a period of exploration of her physical and social environment. During this period of development the boundaries of the world in which she functions start to expand.[38] There is no question that others play an increasingly important role in the child's development. The role of the father is currently being recognized as having considerable influence on the development of the child. Studies have shown that throughout infancy and the stages that follow, father–child interaction differs from that of the mother and child.[39] Bower[40] refers to the mediating effects of the family, recognizing that, in fact, the child is part of a larger interacting network in which there may be multiple, supportive, mediating adults who affect the child's cognitive growth. Garbarino[41] describes the influence of the family, the community, and the larger social system on the child. The important contribution that siblings make to early development has been cited by Bowlby,[42] who sees their role as both attachment figures and as role models. While for young children interpersonal interactions are generally limited to one person at a time, it is also evident that reliable interactions with a number of trusted individuals enhance the developmental process.

Sociability, activity, and vigor are paramount characteristics of the preschool child. Their increasing physical mobility allows them to explore the environment and expand their social boundaries. Erikson[43] refers to this stage as one of initiative in which the child's exuberance spurs her on to new activities and discoveries. Within this stage there is considerable variance. Ames and Ilg note that in general the three-and-a-half-year-old child is experiencing a stormy phase in which she is oppositional, anxious, determined and self-willed, and insecure. They further state that a four-year-old can be considered out of bounds: active, demanding, sociable, and periodically evidencing impulsivity. By four and a half this characteristic has diminished, and at five the child evidences improved self-control and is considerably more mild mannered and tractable.[44]

The results of the psychosocial developmental sequence have important implications for child abuse prevention programs, as the majority of the program concepts address interactions with a child's primary attachment figures. The application of these concepts is to some extent contingent on the child's successful completion of each stage, with a particular reference to development of trust, autonomy, and initiative.

Preschool Learning Environments

In addition to the level of cognitive development, a child's capacity to learn is highly dependent on the interaction between the child and the learning environment. While recognizing the vital importance of the home in the child's learning process, this discussion will focus on the preschool setting and the conditions conducive to optimal learning at the preschool level.

As noted earlier, Piaget referred to the preschool stage of cognitive development as preoperational,[45] a term that indicates that the child has not yet reached the point at which she can manipulate multiple conceptual dimensions. Preschool children learn experientially—through exploration, manipulation, repetition, action, and interaction.[46] Individual and small group experiences are the optimal arrangements for learning at this stage. Retention of new concepts by preschoolers requires gradual introduction and regular exposure. Their attention spans are short, and therefore age appropriate presentations must remain brief.

Learning depends on readiness.[47] Equally importantly, it must be placed in a familiar and meaningful context.[48] The young child will rarely attend to a task in which she has no interest.[49] Play is a dominant mode of learning at the preschool level. While the term *play* tends to have a lighthearted connotation, it is often a serious matter for the young child, who uses it as a means to explore the environment and personal interrelationships. It serves as a form of mastery and as a form of expression.[50] It is a powerful mechanism for learning that can be adapted to individual temperament and interests.[51]

The National Association for the Education of Young Children (NAEYC) has delineated attributes for developmentally appropriate programs for children from birth to age eight.[52] In defining developmental appropriateness, the

NAEYC describes both age appropriateness and individual appropriateness, observing that each child within an age group or a developmental stage is an individual with unique personal qualities and experiences, learning styles, and areas of interest or curiosity. Therefore, the young child learns best in an atmosphere that takes her personal characteristics into consideration.

The area of early childhood education is not without controversy. There is concern that the current trend in education for young children is neither developmentally appropriate nor serving the best interests or the needs of the children.[53] This viewpoint suggests that programs are designed to serve the needs of parents and teachers by encouraging tangible signs of traditional learning (that is, alphabet and numbers) before the children are ready to understand the tasks set before them. The NAEYC position paper states: "Concerned adults, who want children to succeed, apply adult education standards to the curriculum for young children and pressure early childhood programs to demonstrate that children are 'really learning.' "[54]

Child Abuse Prevention Concepts Seen in a Developmental Context

As outlined in chapter 2, the prevention programs evaluated in this study offer a number of concepts in common. Six concepts have particular salience across the programs. These are: (1) touching and the Touch Continuum, (2) verbal assertiveness (say no and tell someone), (3) secrets, (4) identity of perpetrators, (5) support systems, and (6) strangers. The preschooler's ability to grasp each of these concepts can be viewed through a developmental framework. Three related areas that were not measured in the CARE Series (chapter 3) but have clear developmental implications are (1) body rights, (2) guilt and blame, and (3) methods of program presentation.

Touching and the Touch Continuum

Touching and the Touch Continuum (a spectrum of touches extending from good or safe to bad or unsafe with a middle range that is considered confusing and may contain elements of each) form the foundation of all the programs. While the format and terminology by which this concept is approached varies from program to program, the touch (a confusing or a bad one) is the focus of concern. If the child feels that she has received a touch that is described with a negative valance, many of the other prevention concepts (for example, say no and tell someone) come into play.

Multidimensional Aspects of the Touch Continuum. Understanding the more complex aspects of either a specific type of touch or of the Touch Continuum as a whole is contingent on the child's ability to handle operational or multidimensional thinking—an attribute that starts to become evident during latency. The limitation that this fact poses in terms of the preschool prevention curricula is that many of the concepts are presented with multidimensional features. Across the programs, the Touch Continuum contains numerous dichotomies:

"Safe touches are caring. They don't hurt our bodies *or* feelings" *and/or* "We like to get these touches from some people, but not from everyone."[55]

"A '?' touch is a mixed-up touch. It's kind of confusing. You may want it at first and then change your mind. *Or,* you may like the person who's doing the touching, *but* you may not like how the touch feels."[56]

"A 'Yellow Light Touch' makes us feel mixed up . . . maybe happy *and then* mad."[57]

The dual aspects of each of the definitions cited are difficult for preschoolers to comprehend. Cognitively, the child at this level is capable of handling only one aspect at a time.[58] Multiple manipulations and assessments such as those needed to make the requisite distinctions develop at a later stage.

Not only are the touch concepts two-dimensional, but they include temporally separate aspects as well. "Yellow Light Touches" may turn into "Red Light Touches"; tickling may lead to molestation. These temporal eventualities are representative of a two-dimensional shift, again beyond the cognitive skills of the preoperational child.

The confusing touch (for example, the "Yellow Light Touch," the "? Touch," or the "Oh-oh Touch") is clearly too abstract for preschoolers. As noted in chapter 3, very few children were capable of describing a situation that would generate a feeling of confusion. The majority of the children seemed to equate the mixed-up touch with bad touches. The few who attempted dichotomous responses kept within the realm of the physical and familiar. In one instance, the bath was described as confusing "if the water was warm and cold. Kind of warmish-coldish." In typical preschool manner the children placed the concept into their own context and then were capable of putting it to use. However, the preschoolers possessed little ability to apply the concept to an interpersonal situation that required recognition of subtle actions and subjective responses.

Rules about Touching. In a move recognizing the developmental attributes of the preschool child, some curricula have been revised in an attempt to clarify the areas in which touching can be particularly harmful. These programs have become rule-oriented and explicit about situations that warrant immediate report to a trusted individual. One curriculum uses the term *unsafe touches* to describe "touches which hurt our bodies or our feelings."[59] The characterization appeals to the child's ability to recognize a moral transgression based primarily on physical consequences. Another, while also referring to a general category of "Red Light Touches," states clearly that "private parts touches" are bad unless they occur under specific circumstances related to hygiene or health care.[60] These approaches recognize the child's tendency to accept external sanctions for governing her actions. The relative aspects of touching are removed, and the child is given an absolute rule to follow. However, the absolute rules cannot help the child interpret a friendly pat on the behind, a touch on the chest while being picked up and hugged, and other physical contact in which the intention and consequences have nothing to do with sexual abuse.

In examining the developmental implications of the Touch Continuum at the preschool level, the connection with Piaget's theory that young children see morality in quantitative terms rather than qualitative terms (that is, motives and intentions) becomes evident. Children tend to attribute good qualities to those who initiate incidents with an outcome they view as positive. Thus, where the molestation consists of gentle fondling and kind, reassuring messages, the young child may be unable to sense the danger inherent in the situation or in the other person's motives.[61] Prevention programs try to communicate a rule of conventional morality to children regarding touches. This rule is defined not by intrinsic feelings associated with a touch, but by the prescription of adult authorities. When sexual abuse occurs, the child is faced with two contradictory rules of conventional morality—one defined by the curriculum presenter, who states that the touch is unacceptable, and one from the perpetrator, who insists that the touch is acceptable.

Verbal Assertiveness

An important lesson taught to preschoolers involves assertiveness: "Say no and tell someone." The message here is that, should a child sense that a touch is bad or even merely unpleasant, she should firmly tell the other person to stop and report the transgression to another, trusted individual. This message is not easily absorbed by the preschool child, whose behavior tends to be governed by objective morality,[62] wherein the authoritative word of her elders holds sway over her verbal and physical actions. This is especially true at times of inner confusion or turmoil. The preschool child's natural orientation is toward obedience and the avoidance of punishment.[63]

Perpetrators, usually individuals known to the child, often take advantage of their position with threatening statements designed to keep the child from telling. The child's developmentally appropriate behavior will not likely be altered by the brief statement of the curriculum presenters. The child cannot be obedient to all older authorities and is most likely to be persuaded by those having the greatest influence. If, in the instance of sexual abuse, the offender is a family member or one of the child's primary caretaking figures, the child may have great difficulty rebuffing the action or opposing the perpetrator's cautions regarding secrecy. Piaget addressed this point when he wrote:

> Any act that shows obedience to a rule or an adult, regardless of what he may command, is good. . . . The good, therefore, is rigidly defined by obedience. . . . This only points to (the child's) real defenselessness against his surroundings. The adult and the older child have complete power over him.[64]

As noted in the discussion of psychosocial development, the caretaking figures are vitally important in a preschooler's life. While starting to strive for greater independence, the dependent aspects of her personality remain strong. Thus, when informed that there are circumstances in which she should disobey an important adult figure in her life, the preschool child is likely to find it difficult to understand and act on this lesson.

It has been reported that perpetrators may tell the child that if she tells anyone, her mother will no longer love her.[65] These are strong and fear-inducing words. In studies investigating children's reactions to their parents' divorce, it was found that preschoolers were profoundly affected by the experience.[66] One study, which looked at children of divorced families from a developmental perspective, observed that preschool children strongly feared a loss of parental nurturance and protection.[67] This is understandable. Preschoolers are dependent on parents or substitute caretakers for the majority of their basic needs. The developmental task of the preschooler is to gradually shift parts of her focus and allegiance away from the home base. This is more readily achieved, however, if there is a firm home base away from which the child can wander and to which she can return. Thus, developmental considerations raise a serious question about the appropriateness of prevention lessons that instruct young children to be assertive with and even disobey their adult caretakers, a practice that runs counter to preschoolers' natural inclinations and level of understanding.

Secrets

Similar to touches, the concept of secrets has several dimensions. Good secrets are synonymous with surprises such as gifts or parties—messages that will eventually make the other person happy—and should be kept. Bad secrets, like bad touches, should be reported immediately to a trusted adult. The prevention programs' definitions and instructions regarding secrets are generally beyond the cognitive abilities of preschool children. The comments and provisos pertaining to lessons about touching are in many ways applicable to the concept of secrets.

Beyond the child's confusion in trying to distinguish between different types of secrets and to act appropriately is a more fundamental issue: How do children define a secret? Responses from several preschoolers suggest that they may consider a secret to be the concrete act of whispering often unintelligible messages into the ear of another person, with the content of the secret appearing, perhaps, as secondary to the ritualistic act of communicating it. If this is the case, and it certainly warrants further investigation, the message of the programs is not directed toward the children's understanding of the phenomenon. In reality the secrets surrounding an abusive situation are of a more sophisticated nature than is readily grasped by a young child.

Perpetrators

Most programs convey the message that children may be abused by family members, other familiar adults, and strangers. As previously noted, the preschooler is highly dependent on adult caretakers, expecting them to nurture and protect her. Introducing the idea that a familiar, and probably loved, person may engage the child in a forbidden act runs contrary to the child's view of most family and friends. The complexity of this lesson is increased when the child also is asked to understand that, of the people she knows, the perpetrator may be a close and trusted figure or a casual acquaintance. Since the preschooler is concrete, absolutist, and unidimensional in her thinking, she is apt to find it difficult to reconcile her form of thinking with the notion that a person whom she considers to be on the good end of the continuum would ever approach her with a bad touch.[68]

Support Systems

The concept of whom to tell when reporting an abusive situation seemed to evidence a fair level of understanding among the children in our study (see chapter 3). Understanding that a parental figure would provide help or solace is appropriate and further evidence that children absorb prevention lessons through their own lens of preschool development. Programs identify other potential sources of help such as police officers and teachers. While the children in our study expressed minimal recognition of these other support figures, focusing more strongly on this aspect of the support system may prove fruitful, as developmentally it is in synchrony with the children's budding awareness of sources of help and comfort outside the home.

Strangers

Most prevention programs inform children that strangers can be bad or good, but it is difficult to assess their qualities by their appearances. Therefore, the major message is that erring on the side of caution and avoiding all strangers is preferable. Some programs define a safety space, which is the distance a child should stay from any unknown person. Sometimes presented as an arm's distance[69] or the length of a broomstick,[70] developmental theory suggests that understanding the concept of a safety space and maintaining the distance is a large order for preschoolers. The practical fact that children are often in situations such as crowded stores or amusement parks where it is difficult to maintain the prescribed safety space between individuals renders this element of the stranger concept highly problematic, particularly for preschoolers, who tend to interpret rules concretely.

Guilt and Blame

In an attempt to reassure the child who has been abused, as well as the one who may be abused in the future, programs include a statement that abuse is never the fault of the victim. According to Piaget, the child's tendency toward egocentrism—the self as central to all action—suggests that events that affect the young child are often perceived by her as originating with her—that is, incidents seem to her to be caused by her own thoughts or actions. Investigation into childhood traumas reveals that children tend to feel guilt and responsibility for other difficult experiences, such as parental divorce[71] and death.[72] The guilt is not easily explained away. It can be a long-term issue that may take intensive therapeutic intervention to ameliorate. Considering the depths to which a child's inner focus goes, the idea that she should feel no guilt or blame for an incident of abuse may be more difficult to convey than is suggested by the reassuring statements offered by prevention training.

Body Rights

All the curricula state that children are the masters of their bodies and have the right to protect and care for them. The extent of the rights identified in the curricula varies among programs. One program goes more extensively into the child's rights to remain safe, strong, and free.[73] These are highly abstract concepts, which are difficult to define within the preschool lexicon. They have no concrete parallel. As one teacher in our study pointed out, the children equated strong with physical strength and had no conception of the inner strength to which the program referred. (She was concerned that the slogan would be misinterpreted and thereby misused.)

The main intent of the concept of body rights is to reinforce the fact that should the child be maltreated in any way, she has the right to say no and tell someone. The quandary for the young child lies in her reconciling the fear of punishment and the need for viable relationships with caretakers with any rudimentary understanding that she may have regarding her rights to body ownership.

Methods of Presentation

In addition to the relationship between the developmental level of preschoolers and the substantive content of prevention training programs, the methods of presentation also bear scrutiny. The size of the group and the length of the training session, for example, are important factors in the success of a presentation. Young children learn optimally when material is offered repeatedly and briefly on an individual or small group basis. The programs are generally limited, however, to one to three sessions of fifteen to thirty minutes presented to either small groups or the entire class. These conditions are not optimal for preschoolers. Further, materials are presented with a limited amount of individual child participation. As the NAEYC position paper states,

> Knowledge is not something that is given to children as though they were empty vessels to be filled. Children acquire knowledge about the physical and social worlds in which they live through playful interaction with objects and people. Children do not need to be forced to learn; they are motivated by their own desire to make sense of their world.
>
> How young children learn should determine how teachers of young children teach. The word *teach* tends to imply *telling* or *giving information*. But the correct way to teach young children is not to lecture or verbally instruct them. Teachers of young children are more like guides or facilitators.[74]

Although the programs work to avoid the lecture image and use visual aids, bright and appealing puppets, props, songs, and rhymes designed to attract and hold the preschoolers' attention, some of the classroom teachers in our study observed (1) that the visual aids and other support materials served as a diversion rather than as an enhancement and (2) that only some of the children were able to participate in activities such as role playing.

Songs also are used frequently in some programs. They are catchy and clever, but words do not always translate into meaning until they are experientially perceived by the child. It is possible to drill children to remember words or phrases or to teach them rhymes and simple songs, but their responses to these tasks may not reflect a true understanding of the information given. While the use of songs in the prevention curriculum is an excellent means of holding children's attention and creating diversity in the program, in learning the words children do not necessarily comprehend their meaning or their underlying message.

Summary and Conclusions

Turning to the three basic questions addressed in this chapter, let us summarize the discussions and the conclusions drawn in light of developmental theory.

1. Is the content of prevention programs developmentally appropriate for young children? The developmental profile of the preschool child offered in the first section of this chapter and the later analysis of prevention concepts and developmental capabilities of the young child indicate that the content of prevention programs is not developmentally appropriate for most preschool children. The programs rely heavily on concepts that require a level of cognitive sophistication these children have not yet attained. They are told of good and bad touches, secrets, and strangers, as well as of familiar and unfamiliar perpetrators. In the category of touches a third dimension is added—the confusing touch. Many of the concepts are abstract and outside the realm of preschool understanding. Among these are secrets, guilt, and body rights, all of which presuppose an ability to comprehend elements that defy description for the young child.

In the area of moral development, much of what prevention curricula expect children to grasp is beyond their level of development. Preschoolers have difficulty with the idea of intent; they focus on outcome rather than process; they are dependent on and defer to primary adult caretakers for definitions of conventional morality; and they are not always able to discern when an actual offense has taken place.

The findings from the 118 children who participated in our study and the vast body of developmental literature reflecting studies of many hundreds of children over many years combine to point to the fact that basic child abuse prevention concepts are too complicated and abstract for preschool children.

2. Are some concepts or lessons more salient to preschool needs and understanding than others? Preschool children have reached a point in their development at which they can name a few people upon whom they rely in times of need. They tend, when possible, to turn to their primary caretakers—usually close family members. However, the facts that (1) they are currently enrolled in a child-care or preschool outside the home and (2) developmental theory suggests they are in the process of expanding their social milieu to include outside caretakers such as teachers lend credence to the idea of employing support systems that include a select group of people outside the home.

A major national study of abuse in child-care settings concluded that one of the more important aspects of prevention is the concept of teaching a child to report aversive, abusive situations.[75] While, in this instance, the study was addressing the necessity of conveying to the child that her caretakers at home would be understanding should she tell them of abusive situations that occurred in the child-care setting, the reverse situation also must be explained. School personnel might be encouraged to listen more carefully to a child who speaks of a troubling situation at home. Since seeking out supportive caretaking figures in times of need is a developmentally appropriate task at preschool age, strengthening the teachers' role in the support network offers a salient line for prevention training.

3. Are the methods of presenting program materials developmentally appropriate for preschoolers? Besides posing cognitive difficulties, the majority of the programs are not designed to provide an optimal learning experience for a preschool child. To develop a rudimentary foundation for future learning regarding prevention, the number of concepts must be reduced, and the form through which presentations are made must take into consideration the way in which young children learn.

The pace at which new ideas are presented and the expectation of learning at the preschool level bear careful examination. Over the past decade professionals from varied disciplines have investigated and decried the plight of the child in modern culture.[76] Many argue that children are being hurried through childhood on a rapid quest for maturity—a quest directed by their elders with little recognition of the developmental process inherent in growing up. While the concern has been directed throughout the general community, an awareness has been expressed that educational settings—the crucible of childhood—are being permeated with programs and attitudes that do not reflect the current needs of children. In a recent study of preschool education, David Elkind observes:

> Early childhood is a very important period of life. It is a period when children learn an enormous amount about the everyday world. It is also the time during which young children acquire lifelong attitudes toward themselves, toward others and toward learning. . . . To appreciate this truth we need to see the early years for what they are and not through the lenses of social, political, and personal dynamics that provide a distorted image of early childhood competence.[77]

Notes

1. Anna Freud, *Normality and Pathology in Childhood: Assessments of Development* (New York: International Universities Press, 1965).
2. While recognizing that the theories and concepts under discussion apply to children of both genders, the female pronoun will be used throughout this chapter.
3. Philip Cowan, *Piaget: With Feeling* (New York: Holt, Rinehart & Winston, 1978); Erik Erikson, *Childhood and Society* (New York: W.W. Norton, 1963); John Flavell, *The Developmental Psychology of Jean Piaget* (New York: Van Nostrand, 1963).
4. Jean Piaget and Barbel Inhelder, *The Psychology of the Child* (New York: Basic Books, 1969).
5. Cowan, *Piaget: With Feeling*.
6. Jean Piaget, *Six Psychological Studies* (New York: Random House, 1967).
7. F. Abound, "Children's Application of Attribution Principles to Social Comparisons," *Child Development* 56 (1985): 682–88; Cowan, *Piaget: With Feeling*.

8. David Elkind et al., "Determinants of Part-Whole Perceptions in Children," *Child Development* 41 (June 1970): 391–97; L. Smith, "Perceptual Development and Category Generalization," *Child Development* 50 (Sept. 1979): 705–15.

9. Margaret Donaldson, *Children's Minds* (New York: W.W. Norton, 1979).

10. James Garbarino and Frances Stott, *Children As Sources of Information* (San Francisco: Jossey-Bass, in press).

11. A. Baldwin, *Theories of Child Development* (New York: John Wiley & Sons, 1967), 244.

12. H. Bengtsson and L. Johnson, "Cognitions Related to Empathy in Five to Eleven Year Old Children," *Child Development* 58 (August 1987): 1001–12.

13. Donaldson, *Children's Minds.*

14. Garbarino and Stott, *Children As Sources of Information.*

15. R. Ault, *Children's Cognitive Development* (New York: Oxford University Press, 1977); Jean Piaget, *Play, Dreams and Imitation in Childhood* (New York: W.W. Norton, 1962).

16. Lawrence Kohlberg, *The Psychology of Moral Development*, vol. 2 (New York: Harper & Row, 1984); Jean Piaget, *The Moral Judgment of the Child* (New York: The Free Press, 1965).

17. Piaget, *The Moral Judgment*, 124.

18. Lawrence Kohlberg, "The Development of Children's Orientations Toward a Moral Order: I Sequence in the Development of Moral Thought," *Vita Humana* 6 (1963): 11–33.

19. John Rich and Joseph DeVitis, *Theories of Moral Development* (Springfield, Ill.: Charles C. Thomas, 1985).

20. Kohlberg, "The Development of Children's Orientations"; Rich and DeVitis, *Theories of Moral Development.*

21. Rich and DeVitis, *Theories of Moral Development.*

22. Piaget, *The Moral Judgment.*

23. Albert Bandura and F. McDonald, "Influence of Social Reinforcement and the Behavior of Models in Shaping Children's Moral Judgments," *Journal of Abnormal and Social Psychology* 67 (Sept. 1963): 274–81.

24. Albert Bandura, "Social Learning of Moral Judgments," *Journal of Personality and Social Psychology* 11 (1969): 280.

25. Eliot Turiel, "An Experimental Test of the Sequentiality of Developmental Stages in the Child's Moral Development," *Journal of Personality and Social Psychology* 3 (June 1966): 611–618.

26. W. Damon, "Early Conceptions of Positive Justice As Related to the Development of Logical Operators," *Child Development* 46 (June 1975): 301–12.

27. M. Laupa and E. Turiel, "Children's Conceptions of Adult and Peer Authority," *Child Development* 57 (April 1986): 405–12; E. Turiel, *The Development of Social Knowledge: Morality and Convention* (New York: Cambridge University Press, 1983).

28. L.P. Nucci and E. Turiel, "Social Interactions and the Development of Social Concepts in Preschool Children," *Child Development* 49 (June 1978): 400–07.

29. L.P. Nucci and M.S. Nucci, "Children's Social Interactions in the Context of Moral and Conventional Transgressions," *Child Development* 53 (April 1982): 403–12; L.P. Nucci and M.S. Nucci, "Children's Responses to Moral and Social-Conventional Transgressions in Free-Play Settings," *Child Development* 53 (October 1982): 1337–42.

30. Judith Smetana, "Toddlers' Moral and Conventional Interactions with Mothers and Peers" (University of Rochester, 1988); Judith Smetana and J.L. Braeges, "The Development of Toddlers' Moral and Conventional Judgments" (University of Rochester, 1987).

31. Judith Smetana, "Preschool Childen's Conceptions of Moral and Social Rules," *Child Development* 52 (December 1981): 1333–36; Judith Smetana, "Toddlers' Social Interactions Regarding Moral and Conventional Transgressions," Child Development 55 (October 1984): 1767–77; Judith Smetana, "Preschool Children's Conceptions of Transgressions: The Effects of Varying Moral and Conventional Domain-Related Attributes," *Developmental Psychology* 21 (January 1985): 18–29.

32. John Bowlby, *Attachment* (New York: Basic Books, 1969).

33. Margaret Mahler, Fred Pine, and Anna Bergman, *The Psychological Birth of the Human Infant* (New York: Basic Books, 1975).

34. Erikson, *Childhood and Society.*

35. Mary Ainsworth, *Infancy in Uganda: Infant Care and the Growth of Love* (Baltimore: The Johns Hopkins Press, 1967); Bowlby, *Attachment*; Emmy Warner, *Cross Cultural Child Development: A View from the Planet Earth* (Monterey, Calif.: Brooks/Cole Publishing, 1979).

36. Mahler, Pine, and Bergman, *The Psychological Birth.*

37. Erikson, *Childhood and Society*; Mahler, Pine, and Bergman, *The Psychological Birth.*

38. Erikson, *Childhood and Society*; James Garbarino, *Children and Families in the Social Environment* (New York: Aldine Publishing, 1982); Harry Sullivan, *Conceptions of Modern Psychiatry* (New York: W.W. Norton, 1953).

39. H. Biller, "The Contribution of the Father to the Mental Health of the Family," *American Journal of Psychiatry* 110 (1973): 177–280; Dorothy Burlingham, "The Pre-Oedipal Infant Father Relationship," *Psychoanalytic Study of the Child* 28 (1973): 23–47; Michael Lamb, *The Role of the Father in Child Development* (New York: John Wiley & Sons, 1976).

40. Eli Bower, "K.I.S.S. and Kids: A Mandate for Prevention," *American Journal of Orthopsychiatry* 42 (July 1972): 556–65.

41. Garbarino, *Children and Families.*

42. Bowlby, *Attachment.*

43. Erikson, *Childhood and Society.*

44. Louise Ames and Frances Ilg, *Your Three Year Old* (New York: Delacorte Press, 1976); L. Ames and F. Ilg, *Your Four Year Old* (New York: Delacorte Press, 1976); L. Ames and F. Ilg, *Your Five Year Old* (New York: Delacorte Press, 1979).

45. Piaget, *Six Psychological Studies.*

46. Sue Bredekamp, ed., *Developmentally Appropriate Practice in Early Childhood Programs Serving Children from Birth through Age 8* (Washington, D.C.: National Association for the Education of Young Children, 1987); David Elkind, *Miseducation: Preschoolers at Risk* (New York: Alfred Knopf, 1987); Constance Kamii, "Leading Primary Education toward Excellence: Beyond Worksheets and Drill," *Young Children* 40 (September 1985): 3–6; Lawrence Kohlberg and R. Mayer, "Development As the Aim of Education," *Harvard Educational Review* 42 (November 1972): 449–97.

47. Ames and Ilg, *Your Three Year Old*; Ames and Ilg, *Your Four Year Old*; Ames and Ilg, *Your Five Year Old*; Bredekamp, *Developmentally Appropriate Practice*;

Cowan, *Piaget: With Feeling*; Margaret Donaldson, *Children's Thinking* (London, Tavistock Publications, 1963); Elkind, *Miseducation*.

48. Bredekamp, *Developmentally Appropriate Practice*; Donaldson, *Children's Minds*; Elkind, *Miseducation*; Garbarino and Stott, *Children As Sources of Information*.

49. David Elkind, *Child Development and Education: A Piagetian Perspective* (New York: Oxford University Press, 1976).

50. Elkind, *Miseducation*; Erikson, *Childhood and Society*; Lois Murphy, "Infants' Play and Cognitive Development," in *Play and Development*, ed. Maria Piers (New York: W.W. Norton, 1972); Piaget, *Play, Dreams and Imitation*; Jerome Singer, *The Child's World of Make Believe* (New York: Academic Press, 1973).

51. Bredekamp, Developmentally Appropriate Practice; G. Fein and M. Rivkin, *The Young Child at Play: Reviews of Research*, vol. 4 (Washington, D.C.: National Association for the Education of Young Children, 1986).

52. Bredekamp, *Developmentally Appropriate Practice*.

53. Ibid.; Elkind, *Miseducation*.

54. Bredekamp, *Developmentally Appropriate Practice*, 51.

55. Kathy Beland, *Talking About Touching II* (Seattle: Committee for Children, 1986), 32.

56. Children's Self-Help Project, *Preschool Curriculum* (San Francisco: Children's Self-Help Project, 1985), IVa-7.

57. Sherri Patterson, *Preschool Curriculum* (Touch Safety Program, Marin County, Calif., 1986), 7. Available from Touch Safety Program, Family Service Agency, 1005 A St., San Rafael, Calif. 94901.

58. Piaget, *Six Psychological Studies*; Piaget and Inhelder, *The Psychology of the Child*.

59. Beland, *Talking About Touching*, 34.

60. Sherri Patterson, *Preschool Curriculum*, 19.

61. Mary de Young, "Good Touch/Bad Touch Dilemma," *Child Welfare* 67 (January/February 1988): 60–68.

62. Rich and DeVitis, *Theories of Moral Development*.

63. Kohlberg, "The Development of Children's Orientations."

64. Jean Piaget, *Moral Judgment*, 111.

65. Kee MacFarlane, et al., *Sexual Abuse of Young Children* (New York: Guilford Press, 1986).

66. E. Mavis Hetherington et al., "The Aftermath of Divorce," in *Mother-Child and Father-Child Relationships*, ed. J.H. Stephens and M. Mathews (Washington, D.C.: National Association for the Education of Young Children, 1978); E. Mavis Hetherington et al., "Divorce: A Child's Perspective," *American Psychologist* 34 (October 1979): 10; Richard Gardner, *Psychotherapy with Children of Divorce* (New York: Jason Aronson, 1976); Judith Wallerstein and Joan Kelly, *Surviving the Breakup* (New York: Basic Books, 1980).

67. Wallerstein and Kelly, *Surviving the Breakup*.

68. Sherryll Kraiser, "Rethinking Prevention," *Child Abuse and Neglect* 10 (Spring 1986): 259–61.

69. *Child Assault Prevention Training Center of Northern California Preschool Project Training Manual* (Berkeley, Calif.: CAP Training Center, 1983) (hereafter referred to as CAP Training Center).

70. Beland, *Talking About Touching*, 34.

71. Wallerstein and Kelly, *Surviving the Breakup*.

72. Elizabeth Kubler-Ross, *On Children and Death* (New York: Macmillan, 1983); John Bowlby, *Loss* (New York: Basic Books, 1980); Susan Anthony, *The Discovery of Death in Childhood and After* (New York: Basic Books, 1972).

73. CAP Training Center.

74. Bredekamp, *Developmentally Appropriate Practice*, 52.

75. David Finkelhor, *Sexual Abuse in Day Care: A National Study* (Final report of Family Research Laboratory, University of New Hampshire, Durham, N.H., 1988).

76. Bredekamp, *Developmentally Appropriate Practice*; Elkind, *Miseducation*; David Elkind, *The Hurried Child: Growing Up Too Fast Too Soon* (Reading, Mass.: Addison-Wesley, 1981); Kenneth Keniston and the Carnegie Council on Children, *All Our Children: The American Family under Pressure* (New York: Harcourt Brace Jovanovich, 1978); Eda Leshan, *The Conspiracy Against Childhood* (New York: Atheneum, 1980); Neil Postman, *The Disappearance of Childhood* (New York: Delacorte Press, 1982).

77. Elkind, *Miseducation*, 71.

7

Normative Implications of Curricula Content: What Should Children Learn?

While California has the most extensive program of early education to prevent sexual abuse, similar efforts have been launched in many other localities. Several curricula models for providing this type of instruction to children are used with various age groups ranging from preschool through elementary school. These models include *Bubbylonian Encounter,* Kansas City; *You're in Charge,* Salt Lake City; *Red Flag, Green Flag People,* Fargo, North Dakota; *Children's Self-Help,* San Francisco; and *Talking About Touching,* Seattle. One of the oldest and most widely used programs in California is the Child Assault Prevention Project (CAPP), developed by Women Against Rape in Columbus, Ohio, in the mid-1970s. Based on a philosophy drawn in part from programs for women, CAPP emphasizes the objectives of individual empowerment and self-protection. Underlying this approach is a feminist perspective on powerlessness plainly expressed in the text of a CAPP preschool training manual: "Women and children share a similar victim status in that both groups are dependent upon another group of people from whom rapists, or abusers, are drawn.[1] Many of the newer programs have borrowed ideas from the CAPP model.

A variety of instructional techniques are employed in these early educational prevention curricula. Different models use puppet shows, live birds, contests, dress-up and improvisation, videotapes, songs, and stories to deliver their lessons. Some programs encourage parents to sit in on their children's presentations and even to engage in role playing; others have designed sessions specifically for parents and exclude them from classroom presentations. In preschool and kindergarten programs most presentations run from one to three sessions each lasting thirty to forty-five minutes. Classroom instruction is usually furnished by outside service providers, except in the *Talking About Touching* model, which involves training schoolteachers to integrate new lesson plans into their regular curricula.

What are children being taught by the increasing number of programs designed to help them prevent sexual abuse? Despite their varied techniques of instruction and designs for parental involvement, the different curricula seek to deliver content that is remarkably similar. Fundamental constraints in working with young children include the children's brief attention span and limited ability to grasp complex ideas. Only a few simple messages can be conveyed in thirty- to forty-five-minute sessions. The basic information that most programs try to get across concerns touching, feeling, telling, fighting back, and dealing with strangers. At first glance lessons such as "good touch, bad touch," "say no, go tell," and "stranger danger" seem to offer the kind of sound advice that might actually help to prevent the sexual abuse of young children. This accounts, in part, for the growing popularity of preschool sexual abuse prevention training across the nation. On closer examination, however, the messages these programs transmit are neither as simple nor as sound as they may appear.

Normative Issues

Beyond the empirical questions of how much knowledge about sexual abuse prevention is being acquired in the classroom and its use, there is a broader normative issue: Are these lessons that young children should be learning? The question of what is learned can be answered with varying degrees of precision by empirical research. The normative issue cannot be settled as neatly. It addresses the social endorsement of values, beliefs, and behaviors that are promoted under the banner of child abuse prevention training. The issue is complicated by the fact that in matters of physical intimacy and parent–child relations, different values, beliefs, and behaviors that some people find desirable will strike others as reprehensible. In assessing the normative implications of child abuse prevention training, we seek to clarify the values, beliefs, and behaviors that are at stake and how they are explicitly and implicitly represented in these programs. With this objective in mind, a content analysis was conducted of five curricula for child abuse prevention training used in California and elsewhere throughout the United States.[2]

Touching and Telling

A considerable amount of material in every preschool program is devoted to discussions about physical contact, the feelings aroused by being touched on different parts of the body, and what young children should do about them. Both assaultive and sexually related behaviors are addressed as forms of touching. Of the two, assaultive behavior is the easier to deal with, but even here complications arise.

Hitting, pinching, kicking, and biting are painful to those on the receiving end. It is not difficult to convey the idea that a bad touch is one that hurts. In virtually every curriculum the uniform response to a bad touch is to say no and go tell. Children are taught to demand that the touch stop and then tell their parents, a teacher, the police, or some other adult. The lesson is reinforced by explaining to children that they own their bodies and no one has a right to touch their bodies in ways that do not feel good to them.

This emphasis on children's rights and feelings represents the philosophical core on which much of the instruction in child assault prevention programs centers. While this philosophy has support from some parts of the community, other groups would lean more heavily in favor of parental discretion to act in what parents believe to be the best interests of the child. The issue of children's rights versus parents' rights enters a sensitive domain of family life. People's views on this issue vary according to the age of the child and cultural, religious, ethnic, and social class factors. Although many people hold diverse positions on this issue, in the child abuse prevention training curricula there is a distinct tendency to give children's rights greater credence than parents' rights. One curriculum, for example, begins with a skit in which three-year-old Vivian tells her mother and father that she feels hungry and asks for something to eat. When the parents refuse, it is presented as a violation of Vivian's right to eat. Not an atypical case, this example illustrates the unconditional view of children's rights expressed in many programs.[3]

Parents' rights, indeed their obligations in caring for young children to set boundaries that may sometimes thwart immediate gratification, are given little recognition in these programs. Often parents exercise discretion about feeding their children, and they may refuse a child's request for food because he just had lunch, is having dinner in a little while, is overweight, or is asking for junk food. Do children really have a right to eat whenever they feel hungry? Do they have a right to eat whatever they feel tastes good? The answers are not quite as simple as the message children receive in these programs. One might say that a child has a right to a balanced nutritious diet, but this concept is well beyond the grasp of a three-year-old.

Obviously, there is a need to simplify ideas for presentation to young children. But in simplifying this material, complications arise, particularly with regard to the question of parents' rights vis-à-vis children's rights. This is illustrated, for example, by the way lessons on assaultive behavior deal with parental discipline in the form of corporal punishment. Does spanking qualify as a bad touch? Is it a violation of children's rights? Should children report this parental behavior to other adults or the authorities?

Among the five curricula analyzed, one program guide addresses the distinction between a spanking given by parents and bad touches. Here teachers are explicitly instructed to point out that a bad touch is different from a spanking and to suggest that children may need to be spanked by parents if they do something naughty or dangerous.[4] The instructions go on to draw a line between a simple spanking and a beating that results in bruises, bleeding, or broken bones. If they are hit so hard that it causes physical injury, children are encouraged to report the incident.

More than just failing to distinguish spankings from assaultive behavior, most prevention programs quietly but directly advance the view that spanking is a form of child abuse. It is by no means an aberrant viewpoint. In the early 1980s Sweden passed a national law against spanking children. Although it carries no penalties for being broken, this law embodies a symbolic consensus concerning proper child-rearing behavior. While many people in the United States also oppose corporal punishment for children, public opinion is substantially divided, and we are far from reaching a normative consensus on this issue.

What children learn in school carries the implicit weight of public authority, and the preschool and kindergarten years are a highly impressionable age. In the absence of a consensus about the acceptable limits of parental discipline, the relatively few groups that are designing and operating child abuse prevention programs thoughout the country would seem to exercise an undue influence on the definition of expected behavior in this sensitive realm of the parent-child relationship. Although parental consent is required for children to participate in these programs, few parents study the curricula. Indeed, the extremely low rate of participation (34 percent) found in the parent sample across seven program sites in California suggests that the vast majority of parents know little about the substantive content of these programs or the normative values and behaviors they cultivate. (This finding may inflate the actual level of participation since the sample consisted of parents who were interested enough to participate in the study.)

If opposition to corporal punishment by parents was all that good touch, bad touch lessons promoted in the way of normative behavior, then those with dissenting views might register a mild objection and leave it at that. To spank or not to spank, after all, is not an issue over which most people get terribly exercised. But more profound matters of social and physical intimacy are at stake, particularly when the discussions on touching move from physically assaultive to sexually related behaviors.

What exactly constitutes a bad touch? In most cases children are told it is how they feel about a touch that makes it good or bad. One curriculum guide, for example, identifies the typical negative of "Red Flag" touches that children receive from parents and grandparents as including wet or yucky kisses, tight hugs, and spankings. These touches are put into the same "Red Flag" category as incest, genital fondling, and other sexual abuses. At several points the curriculum guide reminds teachers to emphasize that it is how the person receiving the touch feels that makes it a Red Flag or Green Flag touch.[5] When children feel they have received a Red Flag touch, they are instructed to tell their parents, a police officer, or their teacher.

In introducing bad touches that are sexual, many programs begin by teaching children to identify their private parts. But there is disagreement about exactly what these private parts should include. The minimalist position defines them as the genitals or the body parts covered by underwear.[6] A more expansive view includes the mouth and chest.[7] And in some programs physical contact on any part of the body that does not feel good is a bad touch.[8] One curriculum, for example, has the presenter explicitly acknowledge that the hair is not a private part, while another uses role playing in which a four-year-old girl is congratulated for informing her teacher about the next-door neighbor, who sometimes invites her into his house for milk and cookies and touches her hair.[9] Thus, in the most inclusive view of bad touches, children are taught that even a pat on the head could be cause for reporting the touch to the authorities. From this perspective, all-embracing in every sense, the children's intuition—how they feel about gentle physical contact anywhere—is the essential determinant for separating good and bad touches.

This is clearly the dominant perspective found in preschool curricula for child abuse prevention training, although in some cases, such as the *Talking About Touching* guide, children are told that if "someone touches them very gently on their private parts and it feels nice," this is still a bad touch.[10] In contrast, the Children's Self-Help curriculum takes the view that "no one should touch you in private parts of your body if it feels funny or you don't like it."[11] In this case, presumably, if it feels nice, it is all right.

Talking About Touching is among the more popular curricula in the country. The latest revision of this program guide includes a strict rule-oriented lesson on safe and unsafe touches in addition to the conventional reliance on children's feelings. The rule is simply that no part of the body covered by a bathing suit (with tops for girls) should ever be touched by another person, except while being bathed or examined by a doctor. If the rule is broken, children are encouraged to report the touch to parents or teachers.[12] It is no doubt physically possible for a parent to pick up his or her four-year-old daughter for a hug or hold her on his or her lap without touching the child's chest—if the parent's hands are carefully placed under the child's arms and his or her fingers do not stray an inch. But if anyone were to take this rule seriously, it would certainly induce the avoidance of physical contact.

In 1986 the superintendent of the Waukegan (Illinois) School District warned his seven hundred teachers not to touch their twelve thousand students in any way, fearing that a hug or a pat on the back might bring accusations of sexual abuse in the classroom. This advice met with sharp criticism from child-care experts and community leaders. "Touching and hugging," in the words of a PTA leader, "is an indication that love is present."[13] But children are being taught that this is so only if it feels good to them. A hug from a teacher they do not like or that they feel is too tight or that they are not in the mood for is labeled not as an expression of affection (even if it comes from Grandma), but as a bad touch in the nomenclature of child abuse prevention training. The school superintendent's warning, which at first appears needlessly insensitive, assumes an almost judicious shading when placed against the text of good touch, bad touch lessons.

Because intimate contact does not produce the immediate pain of physical abuse, some programs recognize that the feelings engendered by kissing, hugging, rubbing, and other gentle touching might occasionally be muddled. Hence, the confusing touch is introduced. According to a typical definition, confusing touches are those (1) that start out okay and end up not okay, (2) in which you like the person but not the touch, (3) in which you like the touch but not the person.[14] When children experience the sense of being mixed-up or confused, they are instructed to respond in accordance to the familiar prescription: determine whether the sensation feels good or bad and then decide what to do about it. They are particularly advised to take heed of the "uh-oh feeling." As one program text explains: "The uh-oh feeling can be a funny feeling inside your tummy or goosebumps up and down your body. Also, you may hear little voices in your head telling you something is wrong. . . . The uh-oh feeling is very important because it can help you figure out confusing touches."[15] As the uh-oh feeling suggests, the confusing touch is really not all that confusing. In almost every example offered, it turns out to be a bad touch that is not instantly recognized as such.

Avoidance and Fighting Back

If children are expected to deal with the threat of sexual abuse, they must be made aware of its possible sources. Who should children be on guard against? They are told, in the words of one curriculum guide, "We know there are two kinds of people who touch children on parts of their bodies when they don't like it or it feels funny: strangers (or people you don't know), and people you do know."[16]

Stranger danger is one of the themes widely communicated in child abuse prevention programs. Children are instructed not to speak to strangers, not to take anything from them, and not to accompany them anywhere. One rule often cited is that when a stranger approaches, the child should always stand at least an arm's distance away from him or her. The reason for this is that it presumably gives the child room to run if the stranger tries to grab the child.[17] It is the kind of simple rule that appears precise, sounds almost scientific, and gives one the feeling that a practical lesson is being taught. It is highly unlikely, however, that a four-year-old will be able to outrun a determined adult with an arm's distance between them, and indeed this rule might encourage a false sense of security that could be counterproductive.

While children are taught to keep their distance from strangers, the dangers thus avoided are greatly exaggerated. In the mid-1980s there was a national crisis over missing children, whose pictures can still be found on some milk containers. At the height of the crisis, estimates suggested that up to 1.5 million children were reported missing. According to FBI figures, however, only sixty-eight children were abducted by strangers in 1984.[18] More than 95 percent of missing children are runaways, and the vast majority of the remaining 5 percent are abducted by one of their parents, usually involved in a dispute over custody.[19] Nobody knows how many children are sexually abused by strangers, but most estimates indicate that 75 to 80 percent of the cases of sexual abuse involve offenders known to the child.[20] The actual rate of abuse by strangers is probably lower than those estimates suggest, since molestation by strangers is more likely to be reported than cases involving family members.

Strangers are not the only potential offenders discussed in the training programs. Family members, particularly fathers, stepfathers, and uncles, also are identified as examples of people who may sexually abuse children. There is some evidence that communicating the idea of intrafamilial sexual abuse makes a serious impression on children. In a study of sixty-three children ages eight to eleven, Swan found that after the presentation of *Bubblyonian Encounters,* which teaches among other things that a sexual offender could be anyone, even a family member, there was a significant increase in the extent to which children recognized the possibility of intrafamilial sexual abuse. Indeed, among twelve measures of change, the largest difference was registered on the question of whether a family member could inflict violent sexual abuse, to which the proportion of affirmative responses more than doubled from 39 percent to 88 percent.[21]

Three- and four-year-old children are unlikely to imagine that their parents might sexually abuse them. To place this thought in their minds is a delicate business. As one curriculum guide observes, "This point needs to be made in a sensitive way that will not overly concern children about responsible parental figures."[22] The example offered in the guide tells a story of a father who touches his daughter's private parts while tucking her in bed. Exactly how to present this story in a way that is not overly disturbing, however, is left to the teacher's imagination. While many parents may find lessons on stranger danger reassuring, one would not expect them to exhibit much enthusiasm for having their children taught daddy danger or that they must protect themselves against sexual assault by family members.

If children are unable to avoid a threatening situation—for example, being cornered or grabbed by an assailant—the programs inform them to scream as loudly as possible. One curriculum also teaches children to fight back:

> You can kick them. Even if they try to pick you up you can kick them. But, you have to remember not to kick them too high or you can fall over. (Doll demonstrates kick.)
>
> You can stomp on their foot. (Demonstrate stomp.) And you can bite, scratch, pinch. You can do anything you can to get away.[23]

Similar to the arm's distance rule with strangers, this lesson may create a dangerously false impression of a four-year-old's ability to defend himself or herself against adults. It is doubtful that teaching young children to fight back increases their safety. While some parents may view self-defense as a desirable lesson of child abuse prevention training, many would be disinclined to have their children tutored in these techniques.

Are We Asking Too Much of Children?

What are the implications of child abuse prevention training? The programs are right, of course, to say that touching can be good, bad, or confusing depending on which parts of the body are being touched, by whom, and under what circumstances. Intuition may be helpful, but even adults have a hard time sorting all this out. How many adults are seduced every day by false promises, candy, flowers, and gentle touches? It is, perhaps, the case that in their innocence, children's intuition is more penetrating than that of adults—the child being father to the man, as Wordsworth would have it—but the evidence on this score is hardly compelling.

Following the need to simplify ideas and the desire to promote the value of children's rights and feelings, child abuse prevention lessons are infused with what some might consider a basic deficiency: Other people's feelings are ignored. The program teaches that the yucky kiss from Uncle Bill, the tight hug from Grandma, or the unwanted squeeze from Aunt Jenny are bad touches. These touches are seen as an infringement of the child's rights that should be automatically resisted and, perhaps, even reported, which at best disregards the deep affection from which these physical expressions usually arise and at worst implies that there is something insidious lurking behind these intimate contacts. Leaning heavily on the intuitive powers of four- and five-year-old children, these lessons cultivate a self-centeredness and assume a confidence in children's abilities to sort out what are often complex emotional responses.

The problem is that, while most seductions of young children start with touch, a pat on the head or the behind, a kiss, an offer of candy, and the like, most touching, kissing, patting, and offers of candy do not lead to the seduction of young children. They are instead warm, sincere, and nurturing expressions of familial love. But with numerous examples focused on bad touches and uh-oh feelings, the lessons do more than transmit a sense of touching as perilous; they try to delimit the normative boundaries of children's responses to physical intimacy in family life. Physical intimacy between parents and children is a touchy business, intensely private, and quite diverse in its expression. The lessons of child abuse prevention training set normative boundaries that reflect neither the diversity nor the affection of this intimacy. Depending on the curriculum, for example, a parent's affectionate pat on the behind to a four-year-old child may appear as an act that either violates the dictim against touching private parts or should be consciously appraised by the child to determine its momentary goodness or badness.

Whether or not one agrees with the views of physical intimacy, children's rights, self-defense, and strangers presented in child abuse prevention training, and whether or not one believes that the cognitive development of preschoolers allows them to make sense of this training, there is a more fundamental question raised by these programs: Should young children be expected to prevent abuse? At a time in their lives when it is important to have a sense of trust that parents and care givers will nurture and protect them, should children be taught that they must evaluate the boundaries of appropriate adult behavior? The underlying message in the empowerment of four-year-olds is that they must take charge to control the dangerous outside world. It is an abdication of family and societal responsibility—a sorry message of these times.

But real dangers exist. Unfortunately, children are at some risk of serious physical and emotional injury from parents and other adults who are not to be trusted—whose unwanted touches are not innocent expressions of affection. The issue clearly merits further discussion if we are to prevent serious harm from being done to a few with the least damage inadvertently caused by complex messages to all young children, including those who will not understand the intent and those whose sense of trust may already be damaged. We need to find a proper balance, which should probably include placing more responsibility on adults to nurture and protect children and less emphasis on preschoolers exerting their power to correct a situation that the adults in our society have created and need to go a long way toward correcting.

Notes

1. *Child Assault Prevention Training Center of Northern California Preschool Project Training Manual* (Berkeley, Calif.: CAP Training Center, 1983).

2. Children's Self-Help Project, *Preschool Curriculum* (San Francisco: Children's Self-Help Project, 1985); *Child Sexual Abuse Prevention Education Program* (Mimeo, Rape Crisis Education Program, San Luis Obispo, Calif., n.d.); CAP Training Center; Carol Grimm and Becky Montgomery, *Red Flag, Green Flag People Program Guide*, rev. ed. (Fargo, N.D.: Rape and Abuse Crisis Center, 1985); Kathy Beland, *Talking About Touching II* (Seattle: Committee for Children, 1986).

3. CAP Training Center, 2.

4. *Child Sexual Abuse Prevention Education Program*, 23.

5. Grimm and Montgomery, *Red Flag, Green Flag.*

6. Ibid.

7. Children's Self-Help Project, *Preschool Curriculum.*

8. CAP Training Center.

9. Ibid.; Children's Self-Help Project, *Preschool Curriculum.*

10. Beland, *Talking About Touching with Preschoolers* (Seattle: Committee for Children, 1985), 17.

11. Children's Self-Help Project, *Preschool Curriculum.*

12. Beland, *Talking About Touching*, II.

13. Bob Olmstead, "Teachers' Hugging Ban Hit," *Chicago Sun-Times*, 3 April 1986, 22.

14. Children's Self-Help Project, *Preschool Curriculum*.

15. *Child Sexual Abuse Prevention Education Program*, 5.

16. Children's Self-Help Project, *Preschool Curriculum*, 7.

17. CAP Training Center, 12; Grimm and Montgomery, *Red Flag, Green Flag*, 22.

18. Richard M. Cohen, "Fear of the Week," *San Francisco Examiner*, 9 September 1986, A-11.

19. David Finkelhor, "Sexual Socialization in America: High Risk for Sexual Abuse," in *Childhood and Sexuality*, ed. J.M. Samson (Montreal: Editions Etudes Virantes, 1979).

20. Peter Schneider, "Lost Innocents," *Harpers*, February 1987, 50.

21. Helen Swan, Allan Press, and Steven Briggs, "Child Sexual Abuse Prevention: Does It Work?" *Child Welfare* (July/August 1985): 395–405.

22. Beland, *Talking About Touching* II, 43.

23. CAP Training Center, 12.

8
Protecting Young Children: Conclusions and Recommendations

In assessing the usefulness of sexual abuse prevention training for preschoolers, there are a number of issues about what children learn and the effects of this learning that bear serious consideration. A summary of these issues and their implications provides an overview of the analysis that informs the conclusions and recommendations of this study. These issues may be examined under the headings of four questions.

What Are the Positive and Negative Outcomes of Prevention Training?

This, of course, is the bottom line. Assuming for the moment that children were able to learn all the material presented in the prevention curricula, the usefulness of these programs ultimately depends on how well they can put this knowledge to work outside the classroom. With regard to positive outcomes, there are two levels of prevention: the use of knowledge gained from these programs to prevent abuse from happening and the use of knowledge to prevent abuse from recurring or getting worse. In the first instance, there is very limited scientific evidence on the behavioral implications of training. For practical and ethical reasons, the question of how preschool children's actual behavior will be influenced by what they learn about preventing abuse is extremely difficult to study. To test their reactions would require placing subjects in seductive, threatening, or vulnerable situations.

Attempting to surmount these obstacles, several studies have assessed the impact of sexual abuse prevention training on children's responses to strangers using simulated techniques.[1] Fryer, Kraizer, and Meyoshi, for example, conducted an experiment with kindergarten and first- and second-grade children in which the subjects were approached in the hall of their school building by a researcher posing as a stranger who asked them to come outside to his car and help him to carry in treats for his son's birthday party. The findings revealed that after participating in the Children Need to Know Personal Safety Training

Program, among the twenty-three students in the experimental group, the number who refused to accompany the stranger increased from ten to eighteen; of the twenty-one control group students, eleven refused to go with the stranger on both the pretest and posttest simulations.[2] In general, studies simulating direct approaches by strangers show that child abuse prevention training can increase stranger avoidance by young children to some extent in particular situations. It is unclear, however, whether this skill can be generalized or applied to approaches that are more subtle.[3]

Studies using simulated techniques raise an important issue beyond concerns about the initial deception required to test the subjects' behavioral response to a potentially threatening situation. As Conte suggests, the simulated experience may in some measure desensitize children to strangers.[4] Despite these concerns, the behavioral assessment of child abuse prevention training has focused on the lessons regarding stranger danger because they are the easiest and least controversial situations to simulate for purposes of assessing children's behavior. Simulated experiences to study children's behavior in regard to situations that would draw upon lessons dealing with "good touch, bad touch," "say no and go tell," "yelling for help," and "fighting back" are probably outside the realm of acceptable social experimentation.

With regard to preventing the recurrence of abuse, there is little evidence that training leads to the achievement of this objective at the preschool level. The California experience indicates that many of the programs have a private time at the end of their lessons when the presenter is available to talk individually with each child about the material and to receive any feedback the child might have to offer. Two months after the programs for this study were given, no apparent disclosures were made to the presenters or preschool staffs at the study sites. (Two possible disclosures occurred during the study interviews and were reported to child protective services by the research staff.) In general program providers confirmed that they meet with very few disclosures from preschool children.

It is possible that preschool training might have other positive outcomes, such as inhibiting the activity of child molesters. While there is no evidence on this point, it would seem that ultimately the impact on child molesters relates to their perceptions of the extent to which the programs are effective in teaching children preventive behavior.

On the question of negative consequences, there is again relatively little evidence. In medicine they have a dictum: Above all do no harm. In child abuse prevention training one cannot say with any certainty that lessons such as telling four-year-old girls that their fathers could abuse them, sensitizing children to the negative aspects of touching, making them more self-conscious about physical contact and their private parts, and teaching them to fight do no harm. As David Finkelhor and Nancy Strapko point out,

If children have already had peer sexual experiences (playing doctor, etc.) what sense do they make of it after all the discussion about good and bad touching? Are they apt to feel guilty or confused, especially since the programs are unlikely to give such sex play specific endorsement? How many of the children exposed to these programs get the idea that sexual touching is always or almost always bad or dangerous or exploitive? How often are these programs the first thing to come back to mind when children begin to confront sexual issues later on and do they add clarity or confusion to their thinking? These are all important issues that have not been considered very thoroughly by the educators themselves, not to mention researchers.[5]

But these are more than simply questions for educators and researchers. If the potential for negative consequences for a child's sexual development is serious enough to warrant research, then perhaps parents deserve to be made aware of these possibilities when permission is sought for their child's participation in the program. The lack of evidence on the possibilities for both positive and negative outcomes of preschool prevention training lend a certain experimental quality to these programs.

What Do Preschool Children Learn from Prevention Training?

While it is extremely difficult to determine how well children are able to employ, outside the classroom, the knowledge gained from child abuse prevention training, the question of what they actually learn in the classroom lends itself more readily to empirical investigation. This is not to say that such investigation is without problems. Any research in which children ages three to five years are the subjects is fraught with uncertainty. And when the topic explored with these young subjects concerns sexual abuse prevention, the research design, implementation, and interpretation of findings all present formidable limitations.

On the question of what children seem to grasp from the lessons of child abuse prevention training, the findings reported in chapters 3, 4, and 5 (based on a sample of 118 preschool children at seven school sites in California, along with their parents and teachers) offer several insights regarding the educational impact of lessons focused on touching, feelings, telling, secrets, strangers, and other program objectives.

First, in regard to the way children perceived touching after participation in training programs, there was an increase in the degree to which they associated ambiguous touches (tickling and bathing) with feeling sad, a decrease in their association of these touches with happy feelings, and very little change in the limited extent to which they associated any touches with mixed-up or confused feelings. This pattern suggests that the programs may have sensitized children to the negative possibilities of engaging in physical contact such as tickling and bathing, which on the surface appear neither friendly (as hugging) nor hostile (as hitting).

Second, in regard to the cognitive ability to make logical connections between being touched in different ways and feelings associated with these actions, the findings revealed that a substantial proportion of children could neither give a logical reason why they associated certain feelings with actions nor offer examples of why feelings associated with touching might change. Although children in the experimental posttest group showed some increase in their ability to explain the association between touching and feeling, the gain in making this connection was relatively small, with almost half the group still unable to offer an appropriate response to all four touching scenarios. The children were least able to explain mixed-up feelings and improved most in their ability to link sad feelings and touching. These findings suggest that many preschool children are at a level of development that does not prepare them to absorb fully the lessons that rely on their feelings to interpret good touch, bad touch experiences; in this area, lessons that address mixed-up feelings appear particularly difficult for preschool children to grasp.

Third, in regard to dealing with secrets that make the child uncomfortable, the data suggest that preschool children have difficulty with the idea that a certain category of secrets should not be kept. Prevention programs advise children to report to adults when other grown-ups tell them to keep something a secret—if this secret makes them uncomfortable. While the findings show a small degree of improvement, for most children this lesson does not seem to come across very clearly. The proportion of children indicating that one should reveal this type of secret increased from 45 percent to 56 percent after participation in the program.

Fourth, when children are asked whom they might tell or turn to for assistance in situations where being touched made someone sad or confused, the proportion identifying an adult as the source of help increased only about 10 percent after participation in the program. While the lesson had a limited impact, after training 41 percent of the children still did not identify an adult as the source of help when being touched made someone feel sad, and 51 percent failed to see an adult as the source of help when being touched made someone feel mixed-up.

Fifth, in regard to how children might respond when approached by strangers, the findings show a general increase in stranger wariness and avoidance of unsafe situations after participation in the program. Despite the general improvement on scores in this area, the stranger danger lessons appeared to have only a limited impact on many preschool children. About one-half of the children responded to the stranger scenario in ways that did not avoid potentially unsafe situations in more than one out of seven instances.

Sixth, with regard to other program objectives, an analysis of the parent component reveals an extremely low rate of attendance at parent meetings, and there is little indication that those who did attend gained significant knowledge about child abuse or its prevention.

There are several caveats that must be borne in mind when interpreting these findings. Since the posttests were conducted within a few months of the program, we do not know the extent to which the reported gains in knowledge are retained over time. In addition, the differences between the experimental posttest and posttest-only groups raise the question of how much of the reported gains in knowledge are attributable to the testing effect, under which learning is enhanced by the additional practice afforded in the pretest session and by the interaction between the pretest experience and classroom lessons. *If we assume that both the testing effect and the erosion of learning over time are limited, the best that can be said for the preschool segment of child abuse prevention training is that in a few areas it appears to yield rather modest gains in knowledge.*

This general conclusion is reinforced by findings from other research on prevention programs in preschool and the early grades of elementary school.[6] In a study of eighty-four children from three to five years old, for example, Borkin and Frank interviewed subjects after participation in a training program based on *Bubblyonian Encounter*. The children were asked, "What should you do if someone tries to touch you in a way that doesn't feel good?" Only 4 percent of the three-year-olds and 43 percent of the four- and five-year-olds spontaneously offered one of the safety rules—say no, run away, tell someone—in response to this question. Since this study involved a posttest-only design with no control group, it is not possible to determine what proportion of the children who responded correctly had gained this knowledge from the program. Whatever learning may have taken place, two-thirds of the children apparently were unable to absorb the lessons.[7]

Similarly, in a study of forty preschool and school-age children, Conte et al. found that while the experimental group evidenced a statistically significant increase in the number of correct responses to a questionnaire on prevention concepts, the children still failed to get almost 50 percent of the concepts taught by the program; the preschool children performed worse on all the questions than the six- to ten-year-olds.[8]

Using the *Talking About Touching* curriculum, which involves more than twenty lessons, Liddell, Young, and Yamagishi studied 183 children ranging from forty-one to sixty-eight months old. Program presenters were divided into three groups based on the degree of training they received in preparation for the classroom delivery of the curriculum. Findings from this study reveal that after participating in the program the total sample of children achieved an average score of 47 percent on the curriculum content for which they were tested. When the sample was divided according to the presenter's level of training, the children's test scores ranged from an average of 35 percent for the group taught by presenters with no training to 53 percent for presenters with the standard training to 58 percent for those with special enhanced training. These findings are particularly remarkable because they suggest that after more than twenty lessons children were unable to answer more than half the items on a small test that ranged from zero to thirteen points. The children responded correctly to only about 50 percent of the test, and it is unclear whether they even learned that much from the program, since the study employed a posttest-only design.[9]

In sum, evidence from our study of California programs corroborated by other research findings offers strong indication that child abuse prevention programs for preschoolers achieve, at most, only small gains in knowledge. While the behavioral implications of this training remain unknown, it does not seem very likely that the limited increase in learning would have a substantial influence on behavior connected to the prevention of child abuse.

What Can Children Learn?

When a student scores only 50 percent on a test, the performance is usually considered a failure. But when the entire class scores only 50 percent, one is inclined to question the teacher's ability and the appropriateness of the material presented. The limited gains registered in preschool training raise the issue of whether preschool children are able to absorb the concepts around which prevention curricula are designed. As noted in chapter 6, there is a considerable body of research on cognitive development that suggests much of the basic material in the prevention curricula may be beyond the grasp of preschool children.

What preschoolers are ready to learn is bounded by the limits of their cognitive development. Three-and-one-half-year-olds, for example, have a vocabulary of approximately one thousand words,[10] which circumscribes recognition and use of concepts such as children's rights. They cannot deal well with multidimensional concepts.[11] Thus, ideas such as secrets that are good or bad, unsafe touches that hurt or do not hurt but are on their private parts, and a "?" touch that comes from liking the person doing the touching but not how the touch feels are extremely difficult to comprehend. Indeed, the question mark touch suggests a familiarity with punctuation that most preschoolers simply do not possess. In general, the Touch Continuum is a difficult concept to teach. As de Young observes:

> The source of that difficulty lies in young children's tendency to evaluate morality, that is, goodness or badness, the rightness or wrongness, of the situation on the basis of its visible outcomes, and to make characterological attributions to the persons engaging in that behavior in a manner that is consistent with that moral judgement.

The developmental theory of attribution skills is suggested as a reasonable hypothesis to explain the difficulties that young children have in learning and retaining the crucial prevention concept of the difference between good and bad touch. And herein lies the greatest problem: if these difficulties are rooted in the development of children, then they are insurmountable by the children, and that, in turn, suggests that these popular prevention programs are using as their foundation a basic concept that simply cannot be grasped by young children.[12]

In response to this good touch, bad touch dilemma, some programs have substituted the safe touch, unsafe touch on the untested and somewhat facile assumption that the conceptual distinction between unsafe and bad has substantial meaning to four-year-old children. From a developmental perspective, one of the central problems of the preschool curricula is that instead of being designed around the cognitive abilities of young children, they appear to have been distilled largely from existing programs for latency age children.

What Should Children Learn?

The analysis of curricula content in chapter 7 does not answer this question, but it clarifies the normative issues that are at stake. What are the appropriate boundaries of intimacy in family life? Should children be taught to fight? Should they be told they must figure out whether a touch is good, bad, or confusing (safe or unsafe)? Should young children be expected to prevent abuse? It is unclear how parents and the general public view these and other normative issues raised by the prevention curricula. In the absence of such knowledge, prevention programs have taken it upon themselves to delimit the normative boundaries on matters of intimacy and social relations in family life.

The answers to the four questions posed above do not add up to a powerful support for preschool programs as they are currently constituted. The results of these programs are meager and uncertain. Serious issues about program consequences remain unresolved. In light of what is known and unknown about these programs, it would be imprudent to conclude that they should continue to operate or expand along the course that has marked their development in recent years.

Directions for Change: Study Recommendations

The field of child sexual abuse prevention is on the cutting edge of a movement designed to address a vast social need: to recognize and directly confront the fact that child sexual abuse exists and that measures must be taken on multiple levels to work toward its diminution. The abuse prevention movement is still in a fledgling stage, having gained momentum in the late 1970s. The leaders of this movement and those who have followed with concern and dedication deserve acknowledgment. They identified a problem that the majority of the population found too unpleasant to recognize and, after raising public awareness of this problem, set forth to work toward its prevention.

This study has examined one of many approaches to child abuse prevention: programs presented to preschool children in educational settings. After describing the study and its results, the following question remains: What are their implications for action? Before turning to explore the policy implications of our findings, it is important to recognize that the primary prevention programs that agreed to participate in this study did so out of a commitment to the field and an interest in seeing prevention become an established component of the movement that bridges social policy, education, and child and family welfare. The research team from the Family Welfare Research Group, which conducted the study, shares this interest. It is with this shared concern for the well-being of children in mind that the following recommendations are offered.

It is evident from the findings of the study that some major changes in preschool child abuse prevention programs are necessary if these programs are to serve the community successfully. There are at least two directions for change: (1) a move toward significant revision of curricula for classroom presentations and (2) a shift of resources away from the current model of classroom presentations for preschoolers to alternative methods.

Curricula Revision Based on
the Systematic Application of Knowledge
from Child Development and Learning Theory

If the potential for training preschool children does exist, our findings suggest that the current method is not the optimal one. It is evident that a new curriculum paradigm for preschool programs that acknowledges the developmental level of the children is necessary if the programs are to serve their target population. The children's thinking is concrete and absolutist. They are, appropriately, dependent on the caretakers in their lives—at home and in school or child care. They continue to strive toward autonomy, but autonomy, as a preschool task, still assumes support and firm, expectable parameters.

Considering the fact that simple, concrete tasks such as color recognition take continual repetition before being learned, it is necessary to take a close look at the amount of material offered in a short time and without much, if any, follow-up. Prevention concepts are highly abstract. They are open to interpretation and have definite affective components. Often they address possibilities that are far from the realm of the child's experience. They challenge their sense of trust, autonomy, and initiative. The questions are whether preschool children gain anything from brief exposure to the entire battery of prevention concepts and whether exposure to a more limited—and developmentally appropriate—selection would be more fruitful.

The children in this study did not seem to grasp the nuances of difference necessary to understand the Touch Continuum in its entirety; to understand that a familiar, pleasant interpersonal interaction could escalate into an unpleasant interaction; or to understand that some secrets need to be revealed. These concepts are central to prevention. Further, extensive research is essential in order to fit prevention concepts into a developmental framework—to acquire normative data. Certainly the developmental tasks of the preschool child and the expected parameters of preschool cognition have been defined by many researchers and theoreticians. This information can now be applied to evaluating whether the concepts, in whole or in part, can be modified to the point where four-year-olds can handle them. The next step is to go directly to the children and ascertain their understanding of the concepts. It is important to listen to the children and find out not only *if* they understand the concepts but also *how* they understand or misunderstand them. This knowledge can help direct prevention instruction to the children's level of understanding.

In sum, the time has come to investigate how children experience prevention programs and how they comprehend the concepts. Only by doing this will we be able to establish the developmental norms upon which we can refine the curricula. In designing a developmentally appropriate curriculum, each concept must be carefully investigated to define (1) how the children perceive the meaning of the concept, (2) how the concept fits into established developmental schema (cognitive, psychosocial, and moral), and (3) the point at which children are ready to move on to more complex explanations. Once this task is completed, the concepts must be integrated into a curriculum that reflects the abilities and limitations of the young child, taking into consideration the fact that within the preschool setting a year's difference in age is often associated with very different levels of ability.

The recommendation to revise child abuse prevention training curricula in light of the developmental abilities of preschool children raises two important issues. First, it is unclear whether information and concepts that are developmentally appropriate for preschool children would effectively enhance their safety. Definitiveness and simplicity are required to convey ideas to children this age, but educational materials aimed to prevent abuse call for a grasp of relativity and complexity. Even if preschool children could grasp these ideas, a second issue arises: Should the community expect young children to protect themselves from harm by adults? Preschool children need care and security. They are at a point where trust must be nurtured. Efforts to empower these children may not serve their best interests. In a world where we do not allow four-year-olds to cross the street alone, should they be expected to evaluate adult behavior and protect themselves from abuse?

Shifting the Focus of
Preschool Prevention Training Resources

The second direction for change involves shifting the focus of preschool prevention training resources away from very young children to adults and somewhat older children. Three relevant approaches are discussed below.

Increased Teacher Training. Teachers, by virtue of their consistent contact with children, are in a unique position to observe and evaluate children who may be at risk of abuse or are experiencing abuse. If the community wishes to reinforce adult responsibility for the care and protection of children, the role of the teacher and child-care professional is vital to this effort. The vast majority of teachers have only rudimentary training in child abuse prevention concepts. Child abuse prevention education and child abuse detection and reporting are all subjects about which teachers should be well informed. Therefore, if monies are to be expended on prevention for the preschool population, stronger efforts could be made in designing thorough, mandated training programs for child-care professionals in the subjects noted above. Prevention providers, specialists in the field, could redirect their energy and resources to these individuals, offering in-depth individual or regional training to all staff involved in child-care settings.

Community colleges also could offer a great deal in the way of teacher training. Some colleges and universities are now offering courses in child abuse detection and prevention for social workers and nurses. Teachers and child-care professionals could be included in the newly trained cadre of human service professionals if they were offered appropriate guidelines to enhance their roles in child abuse prevention.

Preschool teachers are given the responsibility for the health and safety of the young children in their care. They play a vital role in providing a safe, nurturing environment for youngsters. Therefore, these adults should be taught how to become more involved in the ongoing education of abuse prevention techniques. Moving away from a sole focus on child sexual abuse, the more general concept of abuse prevention can be integrated into the preschool classroom. Children can be taught that hurting other people, taking away their rights, and using violence, threats, or coercion are all unacceptable behaviors. Children need to learn that they cannot be abusive to others, nor can others behave in such a way toward them. Conscientious and well-trained child-care professionals can teach children how to manage conflict and how to get help when an uncomfortable situation arises. Focusing efforts on those individuals closest to and most accessible to young children in their daily lives may better serve and protect children over time.

Reaching Parents More Effectively. Parents are in the most logical position to convey abuse prevention knowledge to their children and to provide the majority of the protection they need. Abuse prevention is a new component in the role of parenting. It is an area in which parents could use factual information and reasonable direction concerning both the nature of risk and the developmental abilities of their children.

Given the results from the parent component of the study, however, it is difficult to see the particular benefits parent meetings as currently conducted offer in terms of child abuse prevention. The premise of the parent programs is to provide education that will help keep children safe from abuse. The problem is that for the most part parents do not attend these meetings, and when they do there is little indication that important learning takes place. These findings suggest the need to consider some alternatives for reaching parents of young children. Several possibilities exist.

One approach is to find more convenient times and places for parents to attend these meetings. For those who work in large settings, lunchtime meetings in the workplace might afford easy access. Social and religious organizations offer other possibilities. Another approach involves making greater use of the mass media. Television, newspapers, radio, magazines, and videotapes are vehicles for adult education in child abuse prevention training that bear closer examination.

Irrespective of the mode of education, certain concepts should be delivered to parents (and other adults) if training for children continues. Prevention efforts currently focus on teaching children to tell. Little effort has been made, however, to direct adults to listen and hear their child's plea for help. Further work can be done to teach adults how to respond effectively once a child's abuse has been disclosed. Adults can take an active role in asking questions of children, engaging them in conversation, and listening to their responses. Through their daily interaction, adults can watch for indicators and verbal cues that might signify possible abuse.

Many prevention efforts also focus on the child's intuition as a predictor of external circumstances. Lessons that instruct adults about child abuse should place a similar emphasis on listening to the parents' own funny feelings. If a parent feels uncomfortable about his or her neighbor, the child's teacher, or a friend, the responsibility for following through and protecting the child should rest with the parent.

Placing Greater Emphasis on Child Abuse Prevention Training at the Elementary Level. If preschool children are not developmentally ready to benefit significantly from child abuse prevention training, the resources invested in these efforts may be better employed in programs for children who are somewhat older. A more intense educational program for children who are intellectually ready to absorb the concepts and lessons of prevention training will yield a much greater return on the investment of prevention resources. The issue here is to determine how receptive children are to prevention messages in the early years of elementary school, the proper form and content of these lessons, and the grade level most conducive to their delivery.

Conclusion

Which direction for change offers the most promise? Should child abuse prevention curricula presented to preschool children be redesigned, or should the focus of resources be shifted? Given the fact that our findings indicate few gains are achieved by children in these programs, and taking other issues raised by the study into consideration, we would recommend phasing out the training for preschool children and focusing on areas or populations with which prevention programs can register more definite gains. We make this recommendation with the understanding that some providers may experience initial difficulties in shifting resources away from the preschool training programs. However, we hope that they will appreciate the potential benefits that the most effective use of limited resources can have for the child abuse prevention movement.

For those who seek to maintain programs in preschools, we would recommend that extensive research be undertaken to establish developmental norms for prevention concepts, to define the concepts through the preschoolers' eyes and using their lexicon, and to delimit the parameters of a reasonable presentation for young children. How to effect the requisite changes remains a major question. The concepts are complex. They require acts of judgment and application of nuances of discrimination that require cognitive maturity. Even with simplified definitions there is no promise that these curricula, presented on a limited basis, will have the desired effect on preschool children. Work in this direction would, however, probably help preschool teachers and child-care providers integrate prevention concepts into their regular curricula.

As discussed in greater detail above, the responsibility for child abuse prevention is best left to the parents and teachers. We recommend that consideration be given to allocating resources currently used in preschools to enriching programs to train parents and teachers and possibly also community leaders who are in a position to reach others who can work in support of children. Shifting resources into parent and teacher education and awareness programs may be more productive than continuing attempts to teach young children to avoid their own abuse.

In the few years since the inception of the child abuse prevention movement, its supporters and developers have made tremendous strides. It has become a well-recognized, widely accepted aspect of social reform. The movement covers a broad spectrum of children and adults. Resources for this group, as for the myriad social and educational efforts, are finite. They must be concentrated in areas where the greatest returns will be realized. Clearly, few gains are achieved through the preschool programs as they currently stand. The resources consumed by training preschool children might be used more constructively on programs designed to sharpen the vigilance of parents, teachers, and other responsible caretakers in these youngsters' lives. This approach would place the duty for protecting children closer to the family and the community, where it belongs.

Notes

1. See, for example, L. Peterson, "Teaching Home Safety and Survival Skills to Latch-Key Children," *Journal of Applied Behavioral Analysis* 17 (1984): 279–93; Ceryl Poche, Richard Brouwer, and Michael Swearington, "Teaching Self-Protection to Children," *Journal of Applied Behavioral Analysis* 14 (1981): 159–76.

2. George Fryer, Sherryll Kraizer, and Thomas Meyoshi, "Measuring Actual Reduction of Risk to Child Abuse: A New Approach," *Child Abuse and Neglect* 11 (1987): 173–170.

3. Gary Melton, "The Improbability of Prevention of Sexual Abuse," in *Child Abuse Prevention,* eds. D. Willis, E. Holden, and M. Rosenberg (New York: John Wiley & Sons, forthcoming).

4. Jon Conte, "Research on the Prevention of Sexual Abuse of Children" (Paper presented at the Second National Conference for Family Violence Researchers, Durham, New Hampshire, 7–10 August 1984), p. 6. He was referring here specifically to the study by Poche, Brouwer, and Swearington, "Teaching Self-Protection to Children."

5. David Finkelhor and Nancy Strapko, "Sexual Abuse Prevention Education: A Review of Evaluation Studies," in *Child Abuse Prevention,* eds. D. Willis, E. Holden, and M. Rosenberg (New York: John Wiley & Sons, forthcoming).

6. For a review of research in this area, see Melton, "The Improbability of Prevention."

7. Joyce Borkin and Lesley Frank, "Sexual Abuse Prevention for Preschoolers: A Pilot Program," *Child Welfare* (January/February 1986): 75–81.

8. Jon Conte, et al., "An Evaluation of a Program to Prevent the Sexual Victimization of Young Children," *Child Abuse and Neglect* 9 (Summer 1985): 319–28.

9. Terry Liddell, Billie Young, and Midori Yamagishi, "Implementation and Evaluation of a Preschool Sexual Abuse Prevention Resource" (Mimeo, Department of Human Resources, Seattle, 1988).

10. H. Gardner, *Developmental Psychology* (Toronto: Little, Brown & Co., 1982).

11. Philip Cowan, *Piaget: With Feeling* (New York: Holt, Rinehart & Winston, 1978).

12. Mary de Young, "The Good Touch/Bad Touch Dilemma," *Child Welfare* LXVII:1 (January/February 1988): 66.

Postscript

I n the spring of 1988 the California Office of Child Abuse Prevention (OCAP) placed a moratorium on the training of preschool children, prescribing instead that programs at this level put greater emphasis on teachers and parents. OCAP officials had found too many unresolved issues surrounding preschool training. They could no longer publicly sanction what amounted to experimentation with three- to five-year-olds on sensitive matters of physical intimacy and sexual relations. This change was fiercely opposed by a group of well-organized, politically active service providers. It was perceived not as a call for more effective prevention services, but as a threat to the ideological foundations of their programs as well as to their livelihoods. Led by Child Assault Prevention Project (CAPP) staff, this group enlisted Assemblywoman Maxine Waters, the influential legislative sponsor of California's Child Abuse Prevention Training Act, to press OCAP to rescind the moratorium. Their efforts prevailed, and in the summer of 1988 OCAP reinstated preschool training—a triumph of politics over reason that ill-serves the children's interests.

Appendix: The CARE Series

Anxiety Scale

We are going to play a game with this little bunny. It needs you to help it show me about how it feels. This little bunny gets scared or worried sometimes. When it gets very scared and does not like what is happening it hides by putting its hands over its eyes and ears like this (demonstrate) so it cannot see or hear. If it is sort of scared it puts its hands out to the black dots. Its arms are out so it can take care of itself if it needs to but it can still watch and listen to what is happening (demonstrate). If it is not scared at all it puts its hands on its lap and is comfortable (demonstrate by putting rabbit's hands on dots on shoes). Now, let's see if you can hold the bunny's hands and help it show me how scared or worried it would be at special times.

The first two situations are to see if the child has the concept.

Help the little bunny show how scared or worried it would be if:

1. a big lion walked in the door and roared at us.
2. its friend walked in the door to give it a present.

If the child seems to have the concept continue. Otherwise reexplain. How scared or worried would it be if:

1. it heard grown-ups yelling at each other.
2. it had to go to the doctor for a shot.
3. it was walking down the street and a dog came and barked.
4. a big rabbit it did not know walked in the door.
5. its bunny friend came over to invite it to its birthday party.
6. it was all alone.
7. it felt something tickly on its leg.
8. it had a dream.
9. another bunny whispered something in its ear.
10. its mommy said that she wanted to read it a story.

Now we have a story we can read to each other.

Bunny Book

Introduction

We're going to tell some stories about bunny rabbits. I have a special book for us to use. It has pictures about bunny rabbits. On each page the bunnies are doing different things. There are four pictures which show a big bunny and a little bunny together. The little bunny looks like this (open book and show first rabbit). We don't know how the little bunny is feeling. Each page has three faces like this at the bottom (point to faces at bottom of page). This face shows that the bunny is happy and likes what is happening (point to happy face). The bunny's mouth goes up in a smile. This face shows that the bunny is worried, sad, or unhappy and does not like what is happening (point to sad face). The bunny's mouth goes down. This face shows that the bunny is confused and mixed-up (point to confused face). The bunny sort of liked what was happening at first but now thinks that it is not so good or maybe the little bunny likes the big bunny but does not like what the big bunny is doing so the mouth goes both up and down. It's all mixed-up. When I turn the page I will tell you a short story about what the bunny rabbits are doing and you can choose the face that you think shows how the little bunny feels about what is happening and put the face on the bunny like this (demonstrate). Let's turn to the first bunny picture.

Interview Questions for Hugging Picture

These two bunnies are hugging. Which face do you think shows how the little bunny feels about hugging?

Response if child selects one and needs encouragement:
  All right, put it on the bunny.

If the child seems stymied:
  Do you think the little bunny is happy? (Point to happy face)
  Do you think the little bunny is all mixed-up? (Point to confused face)
  Do you think the little bunny is sad or worried or scared? (Point to sad face)

After child selects a face:
  I wonder why the little bunny is _____ . What do you think?
  Is there more to the story about the bunnies hugging?

Possible further questioning:
  The two bunnies are hugging and the little bunny is _____ . What do you
    think could happen to make the little bunny feel _____ ? (Repeat for each
    facial expression.)

Final question:
  Is there anything else you want to tell me about the two bunnies hugging
    before we look at the next picture?

Interview Questions for Tickling Picture

The big bunny is tickling the little bunny. Which face shows how the little bunny
feels about being tickled?

Response if child selects one and needs encouragement:
  All right, put it on the bunny.

If the child seems stymied:
  Do you think the little bunny is happy? (Point to happy face)
  Do you think the little bunny is all mixed-up? (Point to confused face)
  Do you think the little bunny is sad or worried or scared? (Point to sad
    face)

After child selects a face:

    I wonder why the little bunny is _____ . What do you think?

    Is there more to the story about the big bunny tickling the little bunny?

Possible further questioning:

    The big bunny is tickling the little bunny and the little bunny is _____ .

    What do you think could happen to make the little bunny feel _____ ?

    (Repeat for each facial expression.)

Final question:

    Is there anything else you want to tell me about the big bunny tickling the little bunny before we look at the next picture?

Interview Questions for Bathing Picture

The big bunny is bathing the little bunny. Which face do you think shows how the little bunny feels about being bathed?

Response if child selects one and needs encouragement:

    All right, put it on the bunny.

If the child seems stymied:
Do you think the little bunny is happy? (Point to happy face)
Do you think the little bunny is all mixed-up? (Point to confused face)
Do you think the little bunny is sad or worried or scared? (Point to sad face)

After a child selects a face:
I wonder why the little bunny is _____ . What do you think?
Is there more to the story about the big bunny bathing the little bunny?

Possible further questioning:
The big bunny is bathing the little bunny and the little bunny is _____ .
What do you think could happen to make the little bunny feel _____ ?
(Repeat for each facial expression.)

Final question:
Is there anything else you want to tell me about the big bunny bathing the
little bunny before we look at the next picture?

Interview Questions for Hitting Picture

The big bunny is hitting the little bunny. Which face shows how the little bunny
feels about being hit?

Response if child selects one and needs encouragement:
All right, put it on the bunny.

If the child seems stymied:
Do you think the little bunny is happy? (Point to happy face)
Do you think the little bunny is all mixed-up? (Point to confused face)
Do you think the little bunny is sad or worried or scared? (Point to sad
face)

After child selects a face:
I wonder why the little bunny is _____ . What do you think?
Is there more to the story about the big bunny hitting the little bunny?

Possible further questioning:
The big bunny is hitting the little bunny and the little bunny is _____ .
What do you think could happen to make the little bunny feel _____ ?
(Repeat for each facial expression.)

Final question:
Is there anything else you want to tell me about the big bunny hitting the
little bunny?

Interview Questions for Secret Picture

The big bunny has told the little bunny something and has told the little bunny
not to tell anyone. The little bunny looks all mixed-up. What do you think
the big bunny told the little bunny? What do you think the little bunny should
do? (Probe: Should the little bunny tell someone or not?)

Tell:
  Who should the little bunny tell?

Not tell:
  Why should the little bunny not tell?

All children;
  Did the big bunny tell the little bunny a secret?
  Are there some secrets the little bunny should not tell anyone?
  If yes: What are they?
  Are there some secrets the little bunny should tell someone?
  If yes: What are they?

Interview Questions for Sad Bunny Picture

Someone touched this little bunny. The little bunny feels sad about the touch.
I wonder what happened. What do you think happened to this sad little
bunny?

If the child responds:
  What do you think the little bunny could do about it?

If child gives response to second question:
  How would the little bunny do that?

If child does not respond with comment about seeking help:
  How do you think the little bunny could get help?
  Who could help the little bunny?
  What do you think could help the little bunny feel better?

Interview Questions for Mixed-up Bunny Picture

Someone touched this little bunny. The little bunny feels all mixed-up about the touch. I wonder what happened. What do you think happened to this mixed-up little bunny?

If child responds:
  What do you think the little bunny could do about it?

If child gives response to second question:
  How would the little bunny do that?

If child does not respond with comment about seeking help:
  How do you think the little bunny could get help?
  Who could help the little bunny?
  What do you think could help the little bunny feel better?

Interview Questions for Happy Bunny Picture

Someone touched this little bunny. The little bunny is happy about the touch. I wonder what happened. What do you think made the little bunny happy?

Did anything else happen?
Is there more to your story?

I know another reason the little bunny is happy. The little bunny has been sitting at the back of this book listening to us tell stories about bunnies and liked the stories. This made the little bunny happy. Now let's say good-bye to the bunnies in the book.

Stranger Story

Now we have another kind of bunny rabbit story. It's a let's pretend story.

Let's pretend that the little bunny is playing outside its house. Let's pretend that a big rabbit the little bunny doesn't know yet comes walking by with a little pet duck. "Hello little bunny," it says. "We're taking a walk to the pond so my little duck can go swimming before naptime. Would you like to pet my duck before we go to the pond?"

Can you take the little bunny and show me what you think it will do?

No response:
Would the little bunny like to pet the duck?

If so:
Can you help it do that?

If not:
Why not?
Can you tell me anything else about what is happening?

Continue:
The big rabbit the little bunny doesn't know yet says, "Good-bye. It is time for us to go on to the pond."

Now another big rabbit the little bunny does not know yet comes walking past where the little bunny is playing.

"Hello little bunny," it says. "I have a nice carrot here. Would you like to have it?"

Question:
What do you think the little bunny will do? Can you use the little bunny to show me?

Refuses carrot:
> And then what does the little bunny do?
> What happens then?
> Is there any more to the story?

Strong refusal:
> What if the big rabbit asked it to come to its car for more carrots?
> What if the big rabbit asked the little bunny to get in its car?
> What if the big rabbit said that the little bunny's mommy and daddy said that it was all right to take the carrot? To go to the car?
> What if the big rabbit said it would pull the little bunny by the ears and make it come with it to the car?

Accepts carrot:
> Then the big rabbit says, "Maybe you would like to come with me to my car to see all the carrots I have there."

Question:
> What do you think the little bunny will say?
> What do you think the little bunny will do? Can you show me with the little bunny?

At car:
> The big rabbit says, "Get in. See all the yummy carrots. I know little bunnies love carrots. You can have them all. I will take you to see where they grow and you can pick some more."

Question:
> What does the little bunny say?
> What does the little bunny do? Can you show me with the little bunny?

Refuses car:
> Then the big rabbit says, "Your mommy and daddy say it is all right." Then the big rabbit says, "I'll pull you by the ears into my car if you won't get in."

Question:
> *Now* what does the little bunny say?
> What does the little bunny do? Can you show me with the little bunny?

Accepts car:
> What happens then?
> What do they do?
> Where do they go?

At End of Preliminary Testing
for Trial Children and
at End of Posttest
for the Real Subjects

Should the child say that the little rabbit would take the carrot, go to the car with the big rabbit, or get in the car, the following should be inserted before the conclusion:

Let's pretend that the big rabbit drives away alone. (Remove rabbit with carrot.) Now the mommy rabbit comes out of the house to tell the little bunny that it is time to come in for a snack and naptime. (Bring out mother rabbit.) Before they go in let's help the mommy rabbit tell the little bunny what to do if a big rabbit it does not know yet really wants to give it a carrot or take it in its car. (Hold mother rabbit facing the little bunny.) "Little bunny I want you to stay safe so if a big rabbit you do not know yet asks you if you want a yummy carrot tell it, 'No thank you. I need to ask my mommy or daddy before I can take anything from a rabbit I do not know yet.' " (Turn to child. Can you help the little bunny say "No thank you?") "If the big rabbit you do not know yet says that your mommy or daddy says it is all right, tell it that you have to ask us to be sure that it is all right with us. If the big rabbit does not leave you alone or it keeps asking you to take the carrot or go to its car, tell it no." (Again turn to child. Let's hear you help the little bunny do that. Good.)

Turn to the child:

Let's finish our story. Let's pretend that the first rabbit and the duck come back from the pond on their way home for the duck's nap. The little bunny holds its mommy's hand and pets the duck. The little bunny and duck both go home to take their naps (act this out with figures).

Index

About the Authors

Neil Gilbert, Ph.D., is professor of social welfare and director of the Family Welfare Research Group at the University of California at Berkeley. His numerous publications include twelve books and many articles that have appeared in *The Public Interest, The Wall Street Journal, Society,* and leading academic journals. Professor Gilbert has served as a senior research fellow at the United Nations Research Institute for Social Development in Geneva. In 1981 he studied social services in the British welfare state under a Fulbright Research Fellowship and was awarded a second Fulbright Fellowship in 1987 to study European social policy as a visiting scholar at the London School of Economics and Political Science and at the University of Stockholm, Social Research Institute. In 1987, he was awarded the University of Pittsburgh Bicentennial Medallion of Distinction.

Jill Duerr Berrick, M.S.W., is a doctoral student at the School of Social Welfare, University of California at Berkeley. She is also codirector for a three-year study that examines child abuse prevention education materials for elementary-school-age children. She has lectured and delivered numerous presentations on child abuse and child welfare services. Her publications include an article in the *International Journal of Child Abuse and Neglect* and a piece in *Children and Youth Services Review.*

Nicole Le Prohn was raised in Berkeley, California. In 1980, she was graduated from Wellesley College, where she majored in psychology. She received her master's degree in social welfare from the University of California, Berkeley, in 1985. Ms. Le Prohn began her work with the Family Welfare Research Group as a coauthor of a set of manuals designed for the self-evaluation of child abuse prevention programs. She was involved in the research project detailed in this book from its inception. She is currently a child welfare worker in the Family Reunification Unit of the Alameda County Social Services Department.

Nina W. Nyman, D.S.W., served as a research associate on the Family Welfare Research Group's study of preschool child abuse prevention programs and was responsible for the development of the Child Abuse Researchers' Evaluation Series. She is codirector of FWRG's evaluation of elementary-school child abuse prevention programs. She has worked as a clinical social worker at Langley Porter Psychiatric Institute of the University of California at San Francisco, as the director of a child care center, and as a consultant for a large urban child care organization. She received her doctorate from the University of California at Berkeley, where she was a chancellor's fellow in social welfare. Her areas of specialization are cross-cultural child development and the development of research methodology for use with young children. She has given numerous presentations on child development and child abuse to professional organizations.